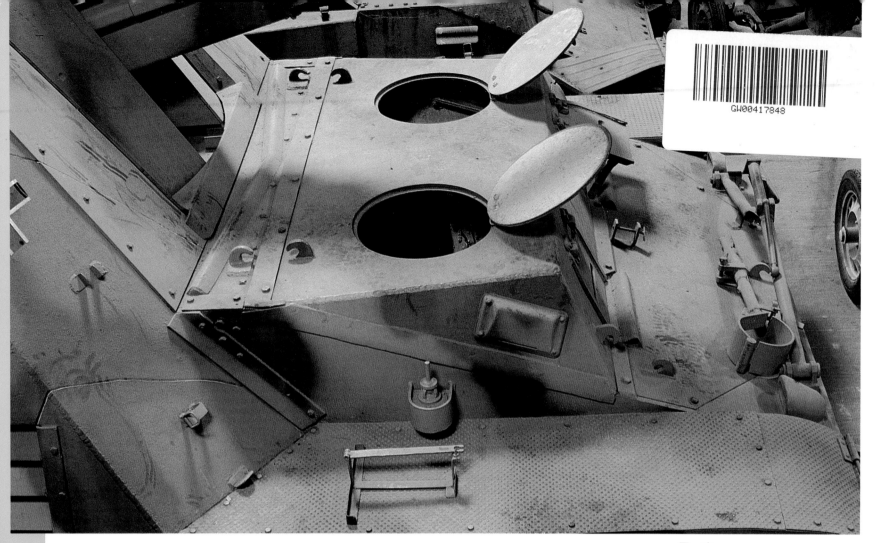

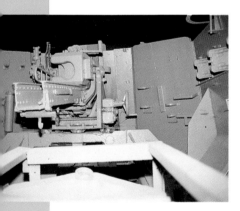

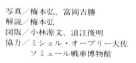

写真／梅本弘、富岡吉勝
解説／梅本弘、
図版／小林源文、浪江俊明
協力／ミシェル・オーブリー大佐
　　　ソミュール戦車博物館

The Publishers acknowledge with
gratitude the help given by the museum,
Saumur musee des Blindes. Colonel
Michel Aubry, director of the museum,
who kindly permitted us to take many
photographs. This book owes much to
the last photograph.

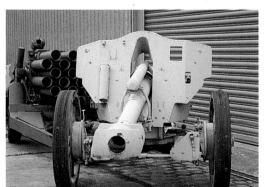

目　次
CONTENTS

GW00417848

15cm Schwere Panzerhaubitze auf Hummel late model 15cm重自走榴弾砲 フンメル後期型

ソミュール戦車博物館のフンメルは車体前部に被弾した跡があるものの、保存状態は比較的良好である。しかし残念ながら現在のところは非公開の倉庫に置かれている。
Saumur museum has a Hummel late model in good condition. But the vehicle is not accessible to the pubic at the present.

ALLEMAGNE - 1942

MEL est le résultat d'un compromis technique

Fahrgestell Pz. III/IV(Sf)(Sd Kfz165)

Manufacturer: Alkett, Deutsche-Eisenwerke		Armament:	One 15cm sFH18/1 L/30	One 7.92mm MG34	Armour (mm/angle):	Front	Side	Rear	Top/Bottom
Chassis Nos.: 320001–	, 325001–	Traverse:	15 left 15 right (hand)	loose	Superstructure:	10/37	10/16	10/10	open
Crew: 6	Engine: HL120TRM	Elevation:	−3 +42	loose	Hull:	30/20	20/0	20/10	15/90
Weight (tons): 24	Gearbox: 6 forward, 1 reverse	Sight:	Rblf36	direct	Gun shield:	10/37			
Length (metres): 7.17	Speed (km/hr): 42	Ammunition:	18	600					
Width (metres): 2.97	Range (km): 215								
Height (metres): 2.81	Radio: FuG Spr f								

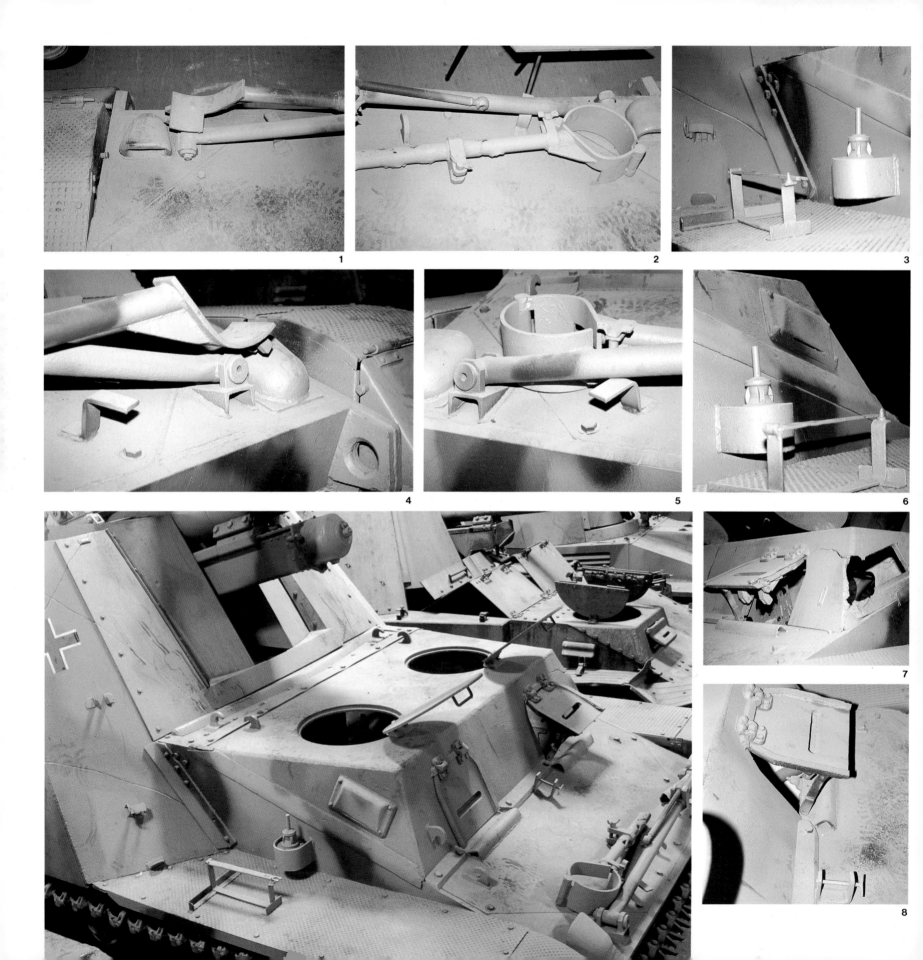

1

2

3

4

5

6

7

8

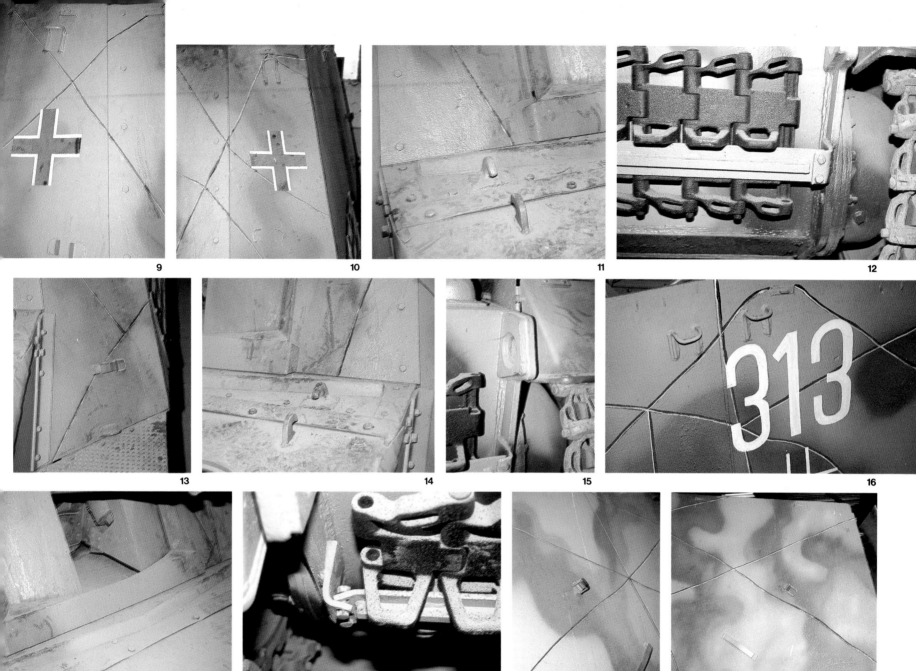

1. トラベリングクランプのヒンジとブレーキ冷却用空気取り入れ口
Folding gun crutch hinge and brake cooling air inlet.
2. 手前のトラベリングランプは途中で折れて横向きになってしまっている
Note the damaged gun crutch arm.
3. 左からバールの留め金、ジャッキの金具、アンテナ基部
From left, crowbar bracket and jack rest block bracket, aerial mount.
4. 左から履帯ケーブルフック、トラベリングクランプのヒンジ
From left, track cable hook and gun crutch hinge.
5. 車体前部の装甲厚は30ミリ、傾斜角度は

20度である
The armor thickness of hull front is 30mm.
6. フンメルは車両間交信用FuG Spr f無線機を搭載している
Hummel was equipped an inter-vehicle communication FuG Spr f radio.
7. 被弾した操縦手席付近
Damaged driver's compartment
8. 履帯ケーブルの留め金とヒンジのついた操縦手用貼視孔
Track cable clamp and hinged visor for driver.
9. 上から幌用フック、乗員用の把手、バール取り付け金具
Top to bottom, hook for hood,

boarding handle and crowbar bracket.
10. バール金具がとれてしまった跡に注意
Note the mark of missing crowbar bracket.
11. 車体と戦闘室のつなぎ目と吊り上げフック
Lifting hooks around joint between fighting compartment and hull.
12. 予備履帯ブラケットと最終減速機カバー
Spare track bracket and final gear housing.
13. バール留め金具
Crowbar clamp.
14. 操縦手室の天井と戦闘室正面下部
Roof of driver's compartment and the front of fighting compartment.

15. 補強された牽引ホールド。フェンダーのスプリングは失われている
Reinforced tow eye bracket. Note the missing fender spring.
16. 戦闘室側面
Side wall of fighting compartment.
17. 砲の真下。跳弾板に注意
Just below of the gun. Note the splash guard.
18. 予備履帯とブラケット
Spare track and its bracket.
19. 左側面のシャベル取り付け金具
Spade bracket on the starboard side wall.
20. シャベル取り付け金具の位置に注意
Note the location of the spade bracket.

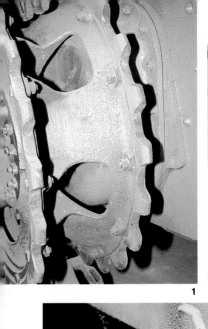

1

2

3

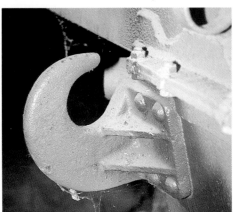

4

5

6

7

9

10

8

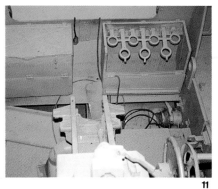   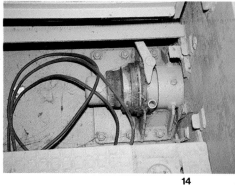

11　　　　　　　12　　　　　　　13　　　　　　　14

   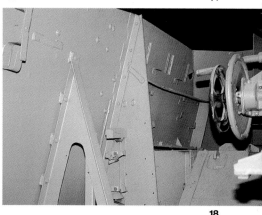

15　　　　　　　16　　　　　　　17　　　　　　　18

  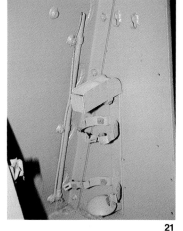 

19　　　　　　　20　　　　　　　21　　　　　　　22

1. Ⅲ号戦車と同型の起動論
Drive sprocket of Hummel is the same model as Pzkpfw Ⅲ.
2. 車体下部側面の排気管
Exhaust pipe on the lower hull side.
3. 車体側面のエンジン冷却気用のグリル
Engine air intake grill in the side wall.
4. 車体後部の牽引フック
Tail tow bracket.
5. 後期型の全鋼製上部転輪
Late steel rimmed upper return roller.
6. 側面から見た上部転輪
The side view of upper return roller.
7. Ⅳ号戦車と同型の転輪
Road wheel is the same model as

Pzkpfw Ⅳ.
8. 履帯ピン脱落防止プレート
This plate was fitted to prevent track pins from falling off.
9. 後部の予備転輪の間には乗り込み用のステップがある
A boarding step is between the spare wheels on the tail.
10. 排気管、後部牽引ホールド、予備転輪。車間表示燈は失われている
Exhaust, tail tow bracket, spare wheel bracket. The convoy light is missing.
11. 戦闘室。床下の誘導輪調整装置が見える
Fighting compartment. The idler wheel adjusting device can be seen in the

floor.
12. 15cm　弾頭庫
15cm round projectile storage.
13. 15cm　薬莢庫
15cm case storage on the port side.
14. 誘導輪（履帯緊張）調整装置
Idler wheel (track tension) adjusting device.
15. 燃料注入孔とMP40機関短銃架
Two fuel filler caps and MP-40 machine pistol bracket.
16. 燃料注入孔
Fuel filler.
17. 15cm薬莢庫（左）と弾頭庫
15cm round case storage (left) and

projectile storage.
18. 消火器架が写真の中央に見える
The fire extinguisher bracket can be seen in the center of this picture.
19. 後部乗り込みハッチ
The tail boarding door.
20. 閉じた状態の15cm弾頭庫
Closing 15cm round projectile storage.
21. 消火器架
Fire extinguisher bracket.
22. 左舷後部装甲板内側のディテール
Port tail wall inside detail.

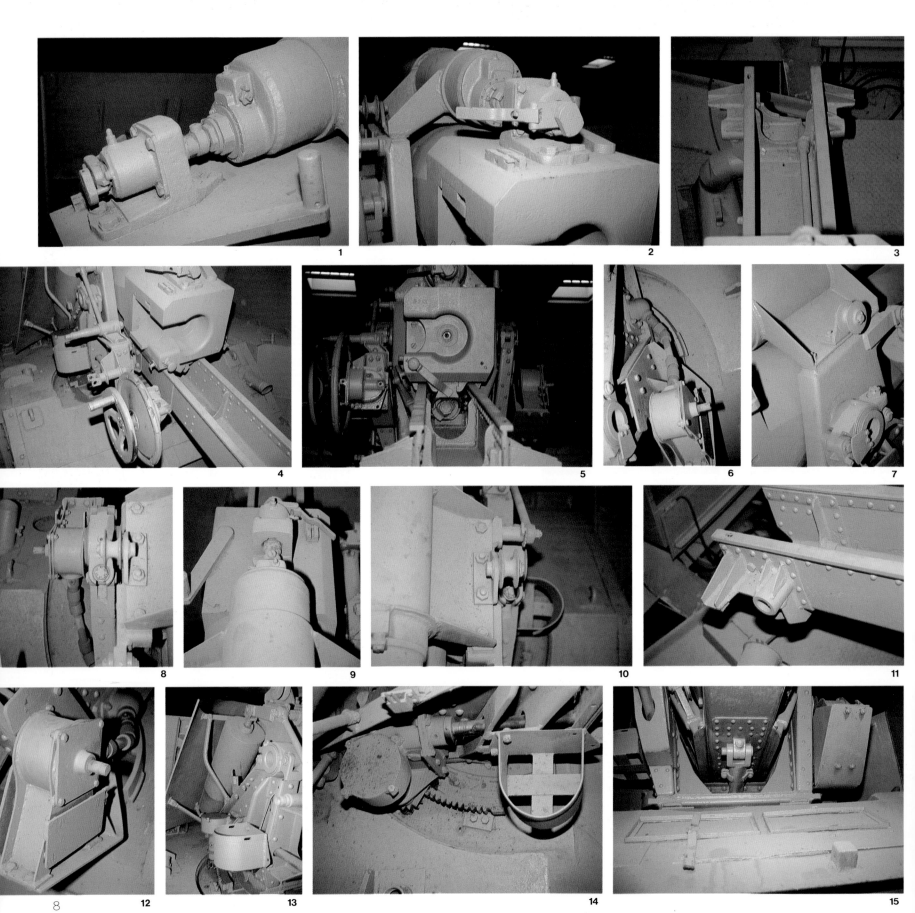

1

2

3

4

5

6

7

8

9

10

11

8

12

13

14

15

16

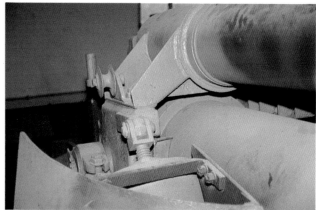

17

19

18

20

22

23

21

24

1. 閉鎖器と復座管ヘッド
Recuperator cylinder head on the breech.

2. 別の角度から見た復座管ヘッド
Opposite side view of the recuperator cylinder head.

3. 上から見た揺架
Top view of the cradle.

4. 旋回と精密調整用俯仰ハンドルが一つの軸にまとめられているのに注意
Note the traverse and elevation fine adjustment wheel installed on a shaft.

5. 閉鎖器ブロックを閉じた状態
Closed gun breech block.

6. 砲手席の反対側に装着されている補助俯仰ハンドル用のギア
An auxiliary gun elevation gear installed on the other side of the gunner's position.

7. 砲耳
Trunnion

8. 装填手によって操作される補助俯仰ギアを上から見たところ
Top view of an auxiliary elevation gear which was operated by one of the loaders.

9. 上から見た閉鎖器。閉鎖ブロック開閉レバーに注意
Top view of the breech. Note the breech block opening lever.

10. 上から見た揺架
Top view of cradle.

11. 揺架の先端
The end of the cradle.

12. 補助俯仰ギア。実際にはこの先にクランクハンドルがとりつけられる
Auxiliary elevation gear was operated using a crank handle which is removable.

13. 砲耳と平衡器
Trunnion and spring equalizer.

14. 左側に見える砲旋回ギアに注意
Note the left hand side gun traverse gear housing.

15. 揺架の底が見える、手前に見えるのはエンジン室の上部
The bottom of the cradle can be seen.

16. 上から見た旋回、俯仰精密調整用ギア
Top view of gun traverse/elevation fine adjustment gear.

17. 俯仰精密調整用ハンドル。旋回用はこの外側に装着されている
Elevation fine adjustment wheel. The traverse wheel is installed on the other side.

18. 後方から見た補助俯仰ギア
The rear view of auxiliary gun elevation gear.

19. 上から見た砲防盾と平衡器
Top view of gun shield and spring equalizer.

20. 防盾と平衡器
Gun shield and spring equalizer.

21. 上から復座管、砲身、平衡器ヘッド
From above, recuperator cylinder, barrel and spring equalizer head.

22. 正面から見た平衡器ヘッド
Other side view of spring equalizer head.

23. 砲旋回ギアシャフト（左）と揺架
Gun traverse gear shaft (left) and cradle.

24. 左舷から見た15センチ砲
Starboard view of 15cm gun.

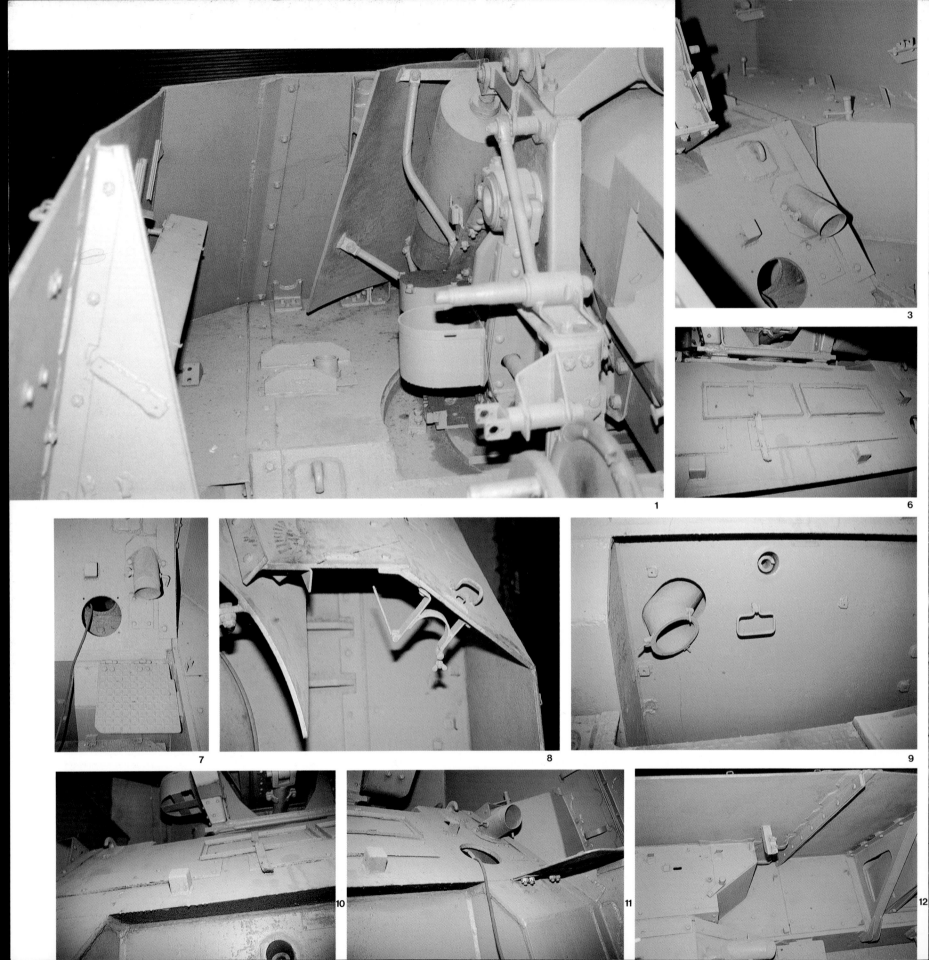

1

3

6

7

8

9

10

11

12

2

13

14

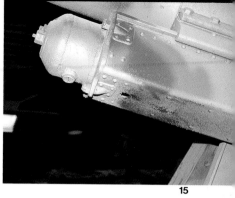

15

4

5

16

1. 15cm砲の左側。Rblf照準器は失われている
Port side of 15cm gun. The Rblf36 sight is missing.

2. 砲手席横のＭＰ40機関短銃架
A MP40 machine pistol rack is beside a gunner's position.

3. エンジン室から突き出た乗員用の暖気パイプに注意
Note the warm air pipe projects from the engine compartment.

4. 砲防盾のクローズアップ
Close up view of gun shield.

5. 砲左側の用具箱、蓋は失われている
Port side storage bin without the lid.

6. 砲架の下にあるエンジン室
Engine compartment under the gun mount.

7. 暖気パイプと装塡手用折畳みステップ
The warm air outlet pipe and the folding step for a loader can be seen.

8. 上から見た右舷防盾
Top view of the starboard gun shield.

9. エンジン室の砲架の真下に当たる部分
A part of engine compartment just under the gun mount.

10. エンジン室
Engine compartment.

11. エンジン室右端
Starboard side of engine compartment.

12. 砲右側。排気ロカバーの上にあるラジエーターの排気調節ハンドルに注意
Starboard side of the gun. Note the radiator air discharge adjusting handle on the air outlet grill housing.

13. 15cm砲身と駐退（後座）管と一体になった揺架
The 15cm gun barrel and the cradle which incorporates a recoil brake.

14. 駐退管には駐退油が充塡されていた
The recoil brake was filled in the brake fluid.

15. 駐退管は砲身の後座を制限し、復座管の機能を調節するためのものであった
The recoil brake had the job of limiting the recoil of the barrel and regulating the counter-recoil.

16. フィンランドのパロランヌンミに展示された15cm sFH18。砲脚の上に装着されている補助砲俯仰ギアのクランクハンドルに注意
15cm sFH18 was displayed at Parolannummi in Finland. Note the auxiliary gun elevating gear crank handle is on the gun trail.

ムンスターのフンメル初期型
Hummel Early model at Panzer Museum Munster

Panzer Museum Munster
Hans-Kruger stra, Be33 3042 Munster
Germany

作図／小林　源文
Drawn by Motofumi Kobayashi

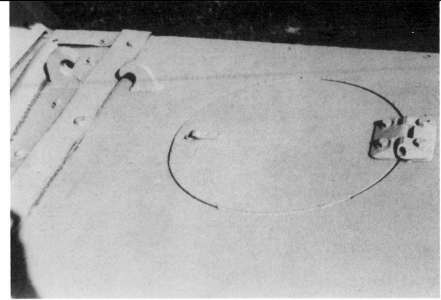

2

4

部分的に開閉できる手榴弾避けのネットを装着した初期型フンメル、東部戦線に送られたSS部隊の車両である
This early model Hummel fitted the openable screen to gaurd against grenade. This vehicle belonged to a Waffen SS unit in Eastern front.

鉤十字の小旗
Small Swastika flag

独特の装着位置の予備転輪に注意
Note the peculiar location of the spare wheel.

観測用のポール
Survey pole

初期型の排気マフラー
Early model exhaust muffler

S型シャックル
S-shaped shackle

IV号戦車の物と同型の泥避けを装着している
The mud flap is the same as PzkfpwIV's.

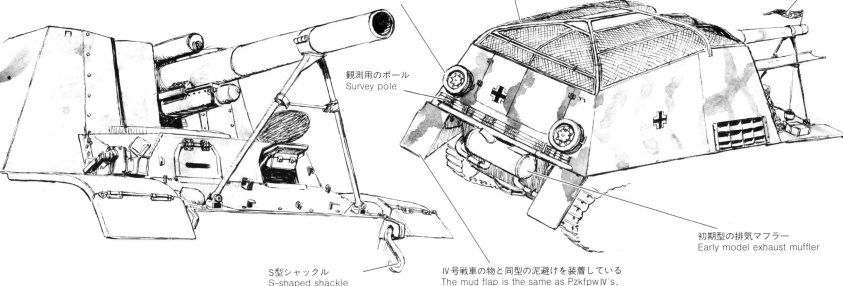

1. 美しく復元されたドイツ、ムンスターにあるパンツァー博物館のフンメル初期型。この車両は完全稼働状態にまで復元されている
Beautifully restored Hummel early model at Panzer Museum Munster. This vehicle has been restored to fully working order.

2. 初期型のフンメルの操縦手室は車体前面の傾斜装甲から突起している。操縦手用視視孔の防弾ガラスは失われている
Early Hummel's driver's compartment armoured hood raised from the glacis. The safety glass of driver's vision hatch is missing.

3. 左舷のフェンダーは博物館で復元したもの。ジャッキ取り付け金具もオリジナルではない。車体前面下部の上部予備履帯ブラケットが失われているのに注意
Note the starboard fender which was reworked by museum. Also the jack bracket is not genuine original. The lower hull front upper spare track bracket is missing.

4. 後期型の操縦手用ハッチ。ハッチ自体の形は初期型と同型だ
Late model driver's hatch.

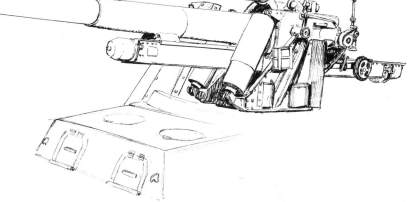

13

フンメル Hummel

作図／浪江俊明
drawn by T.Eiman

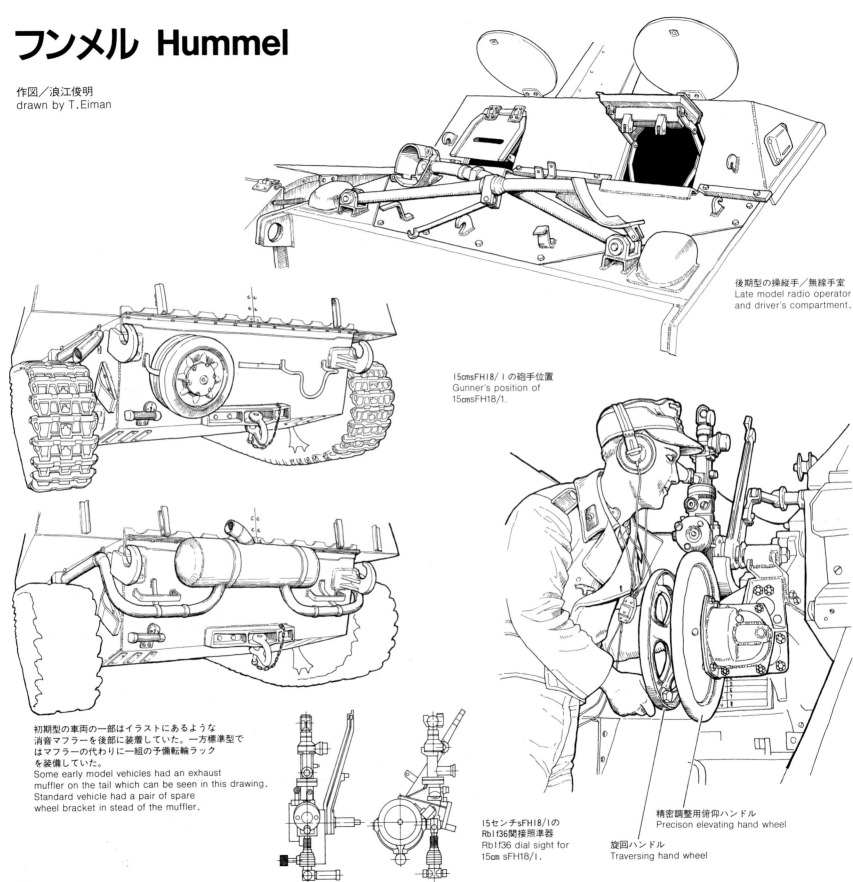

後期型の操縦手／無線手室
Late model radio operator
and driver's compartment.

15cmsFHI8/Iの砲手位置
Gunner's position of
15cmSFH18/1.

初期型の車両の一部はイラストにあるような
消音マフラーを後部に装着していた。一方標準型で
はマフラーの代わりに一組の予備転輪ラック
を装備していた。
Some early model vehicles had an exhaust
muffler on the tail which can be seen in this drawing.
Standard vehicle had a pair of spare
wheel bracket in stead of the muffler.

15センチsFHI8/Iの
Rblf36関接照準器
Rblf36 dial sight for
15cm sFH18/I.

精密調整用俯仰ハンドル
Precison elevating hand wheel

旋回ハンドル
Traversing hand wheel

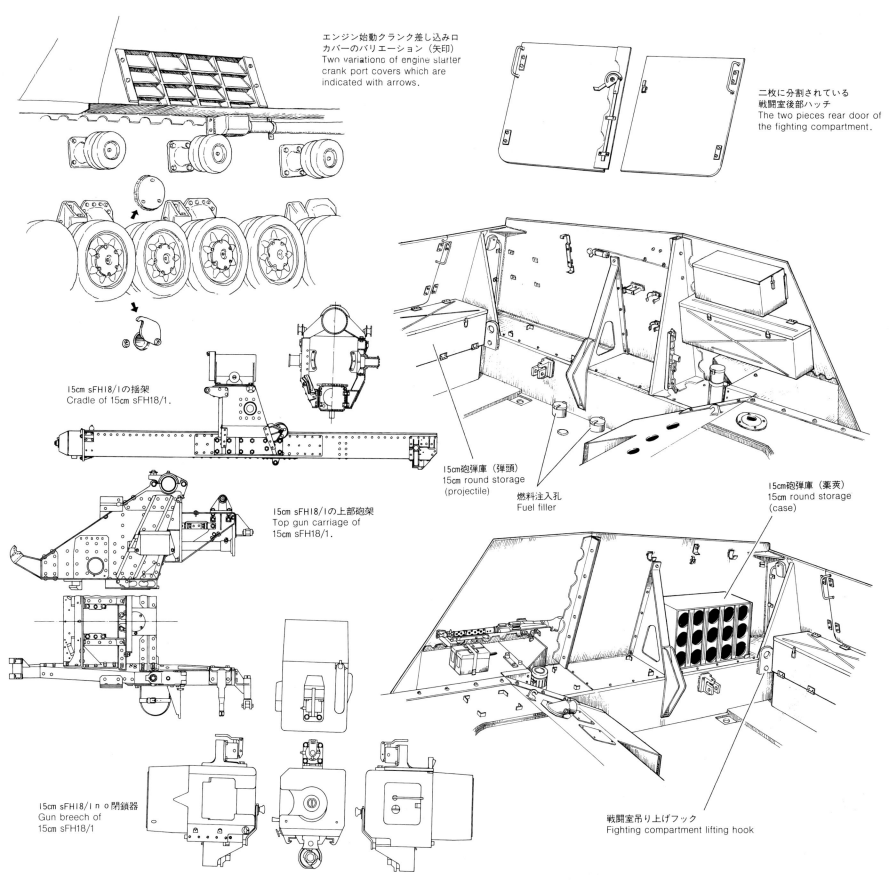

エンジン始動クランク差し込み口
カバーのバリエーション（矢印）
Two variations of engine starter
crank port covers which are
indicated with arrows.

二枚に分割されている
戦闘室後部ハッチ
The two pieces rear door of
the fighting compartment.

15cm sFH18/1の揺架
Cradle of 15cm sFH18/1.

15cm sFH18/1の上部砲架
Top gun carriage of
15cm sFH18/1.

15cm砲弾庫（弾頭）
15cm round storage
(projectile)

燃料注入孔
Fuel filler

15cm砲弾庫（薬莢）
15cm round storage
(case)

15cm sFH18/1の０閉鎖器
Gun breech of
15cm sFH18/1

戦闘室吊り上げフック
Fighting compartment lifting hook

15

フンメル
Hummel

1：35図面
作画／浪江俊明

1：35 scale
drawn by T. Eiman

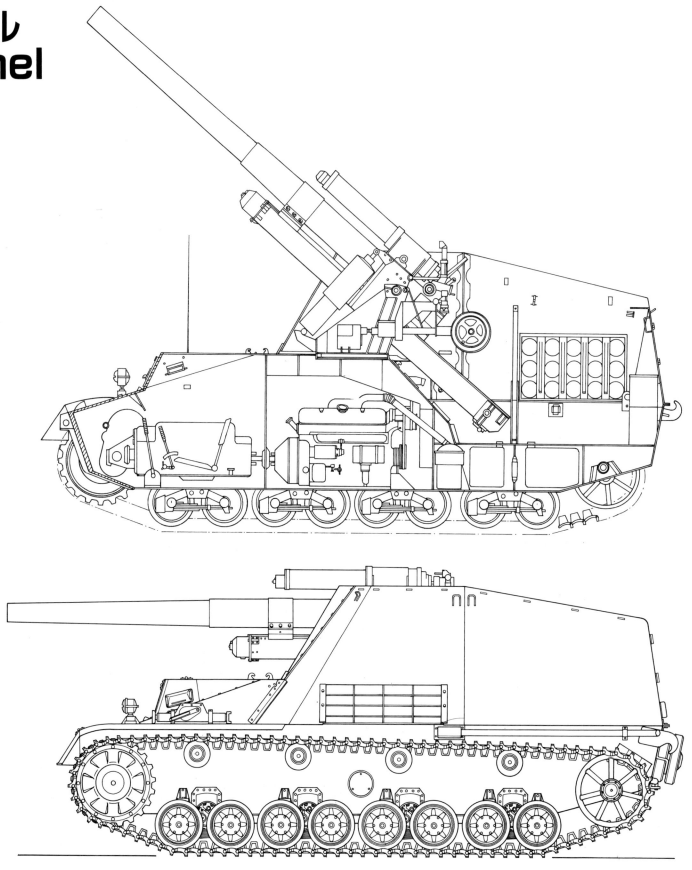

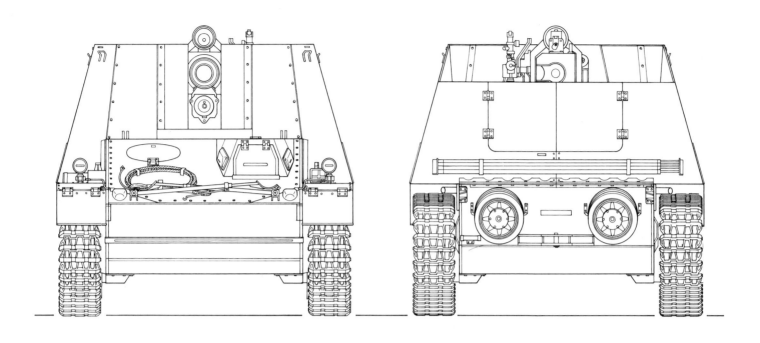

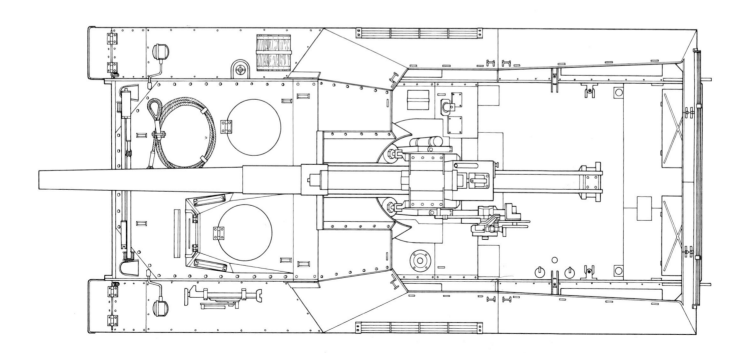

8.8cm Pak43/1(L/71) auf Fahr-Nashorn

8.8cm Pak43/1(L/71)対戦車自走砲　ナスホルン

米国メリーランド州のアバディーン戦車博物館に保存されているナスホルン。野外展示なので状態はあまりよくない。
This Nashorn is displayed at Aberdeen proving ground in USA.

gestell PzKpfw. III/IV (Sf)(Sd Kfz164)

Manufacturer: Deutsche-Eisenwerke
Chassis Nos.: 310001–310494

Crew: 4
Weight (tons): 24
Length (metres): 8.44
Width (metres): 2.86
Height (metres): 2.65

Engine: Maybach HL120TRM
Gearbox: 6 forward, I reverse
Speed (km/hr): 42
Range (km): 215
Radio: FuG Spr d

Armament:	One 8.8cm Pak43/1L/71	One 7.92mm MG34
Traverse:	30°(hand)	loose
Elevation:	−5° +20°	loose
Sight:	SflZFIa, Rblf36	direct
Ammunition:	40	600

Armour (mm/angle):	Front	Side	Rear	Top/Bottom
Superstructure:	10/37°	10/16°	10/10°	open
Hull:	30/20°	20/0°	20/10°	15/90°
Gun shield:	10/37°			

1

2

3

4

5

6

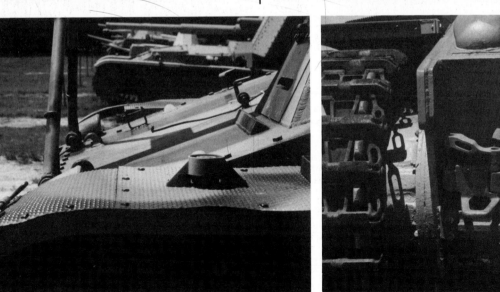

7

8

9

10   11   12   13

14   15   16

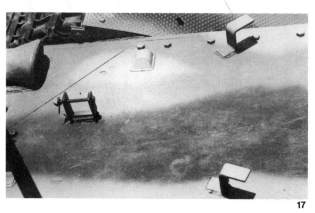

17   18   19

1. 上から見た右舷フェンダー。アンテナ基部ジャッキ台取り付け金具が見える
Top view of starboard fender. Note the aerial mount and jack rest block bracket.

2. 操縦手室とヒンジ付き覗視孔。その横にトラベルクランプ解除ワイヤーが見える
Driver's compartment armoured hood and hinged visor. Note the gun crutch releasing wire beside the hood.

3. 真上から見たボッシュ管制燈基部
Top view of Bosch black−out light mount.

4. 別角度から見たボッシュ管制燈基部
Another view of Bosch light mount.

5. 左から、ブレーキ冷却空気取り入口、スプリング付きトラベルクランプ、前面傾斜装無線手用ハッチ
From left, the brake cooling air intake, the gun crutch with spring, the lifting hook

for bolted glacis armour, three tow cable hooks and the radio operator's hatch are on the glacis.

6. 覗視孔の前には跳弾板が設置されている
There is the splash guard in front of the driver's visor.

7. 横から見たトラベルクランプ。跳弾板の横に見えるトラベルクランプ解除ワイヤーの滑車に注意
Side view of gun crutch. Note the pulley of the gun crutch releasing wire beside splash guard.

8. 最終減速機カバーと予備履帯ブラケット
Spare track bracket and final gear housing.

9. 補強された牽引ホールド
Note the reinforced tow eye bracket.

10. 砲防盾の根元。跳弾板が破損していることに注意

Bottom of gun shield. The splash guard is damaged.

11. 丸い砲防盾と跳弾板。揺架下部の防盾が破損していることに注意
Rounded gun mantlet and its splash guard. Note the damaged shield under the cradle.

12. 揺架の底部、俯抑ギアが見える
Bottom of cradle. The elevating gear can be seen.

13. 防盾上部、復座管、砲身、揺架が見える
Top of gun mantlet and recuperator cylinder, barrel, cradle.

14. 右舷から見た前面傾斜装甲。アンテナ基部とジャッキ台取り付け金具が見える
Starboard of hull glacis. Note the aerial mount and the jack rest block bracket.

15. 揺架の下に見えるのは牽引式のPak43/41のトラベルクランプ用のフック

Note the Pak 43/41 towing model's gun crutch hook is remaining on the cradle.

16. 揺架の先端についている駐退管のキャップに注目
Note the recoil brake cylinder cap on the end of the cradle.

17. 前面傾斜装甲板の牽引ロープ用のフック
Tow cable hook on glacis.

18. 前面傾斜装甲板の無線手用ハッチ
Radio operator's hatch on glacis.

19. 駐退スライドとそのレール
Recoil slide and its rail.

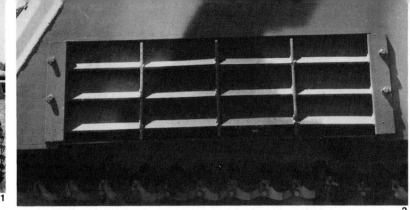

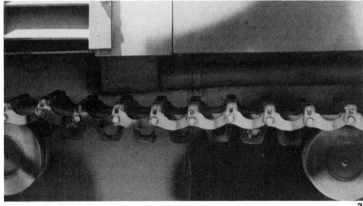

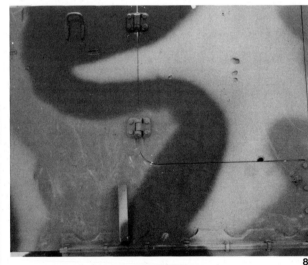

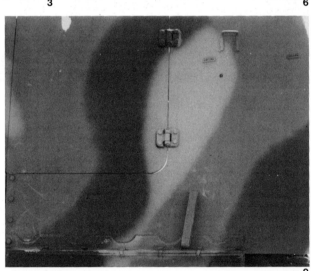

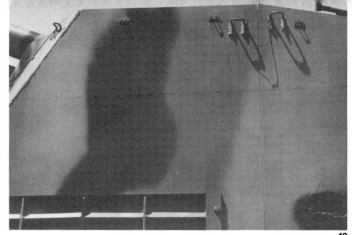

12

13

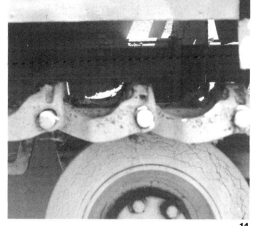

14

15

16

17

18

19

20

1. 車体後部の車体／戦闘室接合ジョイント
に注目
Note the tail joint between the hull and the
fighting compartment.

2. 左舷のエンジン冷却気吸入グリル。空気
は左舷のグリルを通して吸入され、右舷の グ
リルから排出される
Port engine cooling air inlet grill. Air was
drawn into the compartment through the
port grill and expelled through the starboard grill.

3. 戦闘室下部に排気管が見える、これは車
体後部までつながっている
The exhaust pipe can be seen under the
fighting compartment. It leads to the tail.

4. 排気管、牽引ホールドと予備転輪
Exhaust pipe towing bracket and spare
wheel.

5. 上部転輪
Upper return roller.

6. エンジンスタータークランク孔カバー
Engine starter port cover on the port lower
hull side.

7. 排気管はエンジン室側面から引かれてき
ている。その下には覆帯ピン脱落防止プレー
トが見える
The exhaust pipe feeds from the engine
compartment. There is a plate which
prevented the track pin from falling off
under the pipe.

8.9. 上から、乗り込み用把手、後部乗降ハッ
チヒンジ、小さな幌用のフック、クリーニン
グロッド用取り付け金具とボルト留めの車
体／戦闘室ジョイント
From above, boarding handle, rear boarding door hinges, tiny hood hooks, gun
cleaning rod bracket and bolted joint hull
and fighting compartment.

10. 予備転輪の下に車間表示燈基部が見える
The convoy light bracket can be seen under

the wheel.

11. 乗降用ステップに牽引ピントルと予備転
輪ブラケット
Boarding step, towing pintel and spare
wheel bracket.

12. 左舷装甲板、ひと組の乗り込み用把手
と3つの幌用フックがある
Side wall of port side. There is a pair of
boarding handles and three hood hooks.

13. 左舷装甲板後部、幌用のフックがもう3
つ見える
Port side wall with three more hood hooks.

14. 車体／戦闘室接合ジョイントが見える
The joint between the fighting compartment
and hull can be seen.

15. 車体前面装甲板の左舷側板。フェンダー
上にはジャッキ取り付け金具がある
Port side view of hull glacis. There is the
jack bracket on the port fender.

16. 戦闘室側面板と、正面傾斜装甲の側板と

のジョイントのクローズアップ
The close up view of bolted joint on the side
wall of fighting compartment and the hull
glacis side wall.

17. 右舷
Starboard side view.

18. 起動輪はⅢ号戦車と同形
The drive sprocket is the same model as
Pz. Ⅲ's.

19. 転輪はⅣ号戦車と同形
The road wheel is the same model as Pz.
Ⅳ's.

20. 誘導輪はⅣ号戦車と同形
The idler wheel is the same model as Pz.
Ⅳ's.

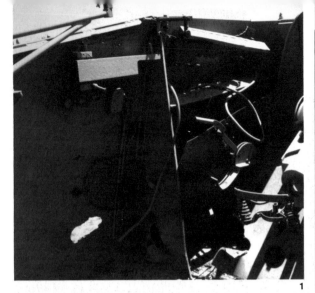

1

2

3

5

6

8

4

9

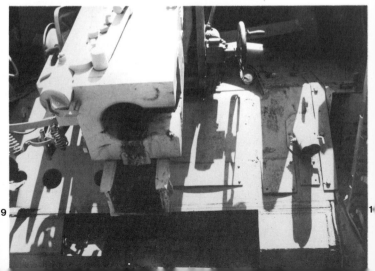

12

15

16

17

11

13

14

19

20

1. 損傷した左舷車長位置付近。画面中央付近に砲隊鏡マウント、ペリスコープマウント、車内燈などが見えるが、左舷の8.8cm砲弾庫は失われている。トラベルクランプ解除レバーが砲手席のそばに見える

Damaged port side of the gun around the commader's position. The scissors telescope mount, the periscope mount and the on board light can be seen in the center of this picture. The port 8.8cm round storage is missing. The gun crutch releasing lever can be seen beside the gunner's seat.

2. 砲手位置。俯仰ハンドルの真ん中に発射ボタンがある。手前のは旋回ハンドル

Gunner's position. Note the trigger in the center of the elevating hand wheel (disk). The spoked one is for traversing.

3. 照準器支持架。SflZFlaとRblf36照準器は失われている

The gun sight support. SflZFla and Rblf36 gun sights are missing.

4. 復座管と2本の平衡器

Recuperator and a pair of spring equalizers.

5. 左舷の対空機関銃架

Port anti-aircraft machine gun mount.

6. 揺架と上部砲架

Cradle and top gun carriage.

7. 誘導輪調整器（覆帯緊張装置）が床下に見える。二つの燃料注入孔キャップに注意

The idler wheel adjuster can be seen in the floor. Note the two fuel filler caps.

8. 戦闘室の装甲板と丸みを帯びた砲防盾

Fighting compartment armour and rounded gun shield.

9. 上部砲架と防盾支持架

Top gun carriage and shield supports.

10. エンジン室と砲閉鎖器

Engine compartment and gun breech.

11. 砲の右舷。装甲板に沿って左からアンテナ基部、ペリスコープ取り付け金具、対空機関銃架

Starboard of the gun. from left along the

side wall, aerial mount, periscope mount and starboard anti aircraft machine gun mount.

12. 8.8cm砲弾庫、蓋は失われている。その隣には無線機ラックと雨避けがある

8.8cm round storage. The lid is missing. Note the radio bracket and its rain shield.

13. 平衡器

Spring equalizer.

14. 照準器支持架。閉鎖器の横には防危板と閉鎖器の上のスプリングケースがついている。閉鎖器の上の閉鎖レバーの把手が折り畳まれているのに注意

Sight support. There is the breech mechanism spring case and the safety shield for gunner on the breech side. Note the folded vertical handle of the breech mechanism lever on the top of it.

15. 8.8cm砲弾庫と後部ハッチ。MP40機関短銃架と弾薬パウチ用のフックがハッチの横についている

8.8cm round storage and rear boarding

door. A MP40 machine pistol bracket and the hooks for the ammunition are beside the door.

16. 後部ハッチのロックレバー。もう一つのMP40用が後壁についている

Rear boarding door with locking lever. Another MP40 machine pistol bracket is on the rear wall.

17. 砲の右舷についている補助俯仰ハンドル

Auxiliary gun elevating hand wheel on the starboard of the gun.

18. 平衡器と砲防盾支持架

Spring equalizer and rounded gun shield and its supports.

19. 右舷の壁についている金具類に注目

Note the bracket on the starboard wall.

20. 右舷から見た71口径8.8cm Pak43/1

Starboard of 8.8cm Pak43/1 L/71 gun.

ナスホルン　Nashorn

1：35図面 作図／浪江俊明　1:35scale drawn by T. Eiman

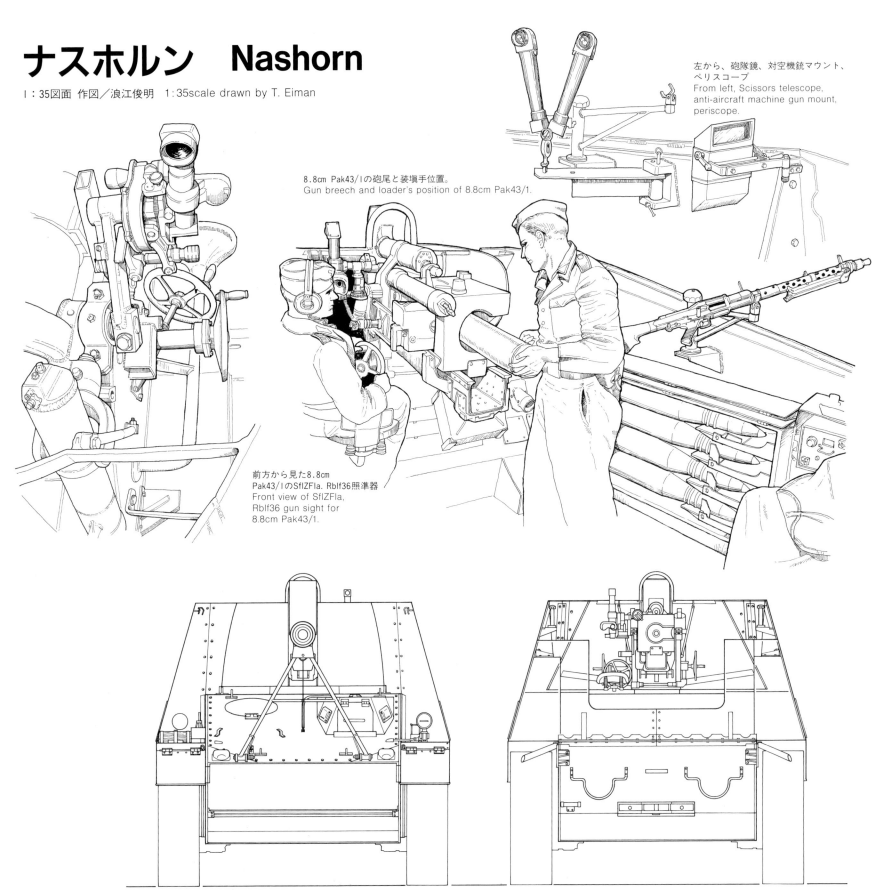

左から、砲隊鏡、対空機銃マウント、
ペリスコープ
From left, Scissors telescope,
anti-aircraft machine gun mount,
periscope.

8.8cm Pak43/1の砲尾と装塡手位置。
Gun breech and loader's position of 8.8cm Pak43/1.

前方から見た8.8cm
Pak43/1のSflZFla. Rblf36照準器
Front view of SflZFla,
Rblf36 gun sight for
8.8cm Pak43/1.

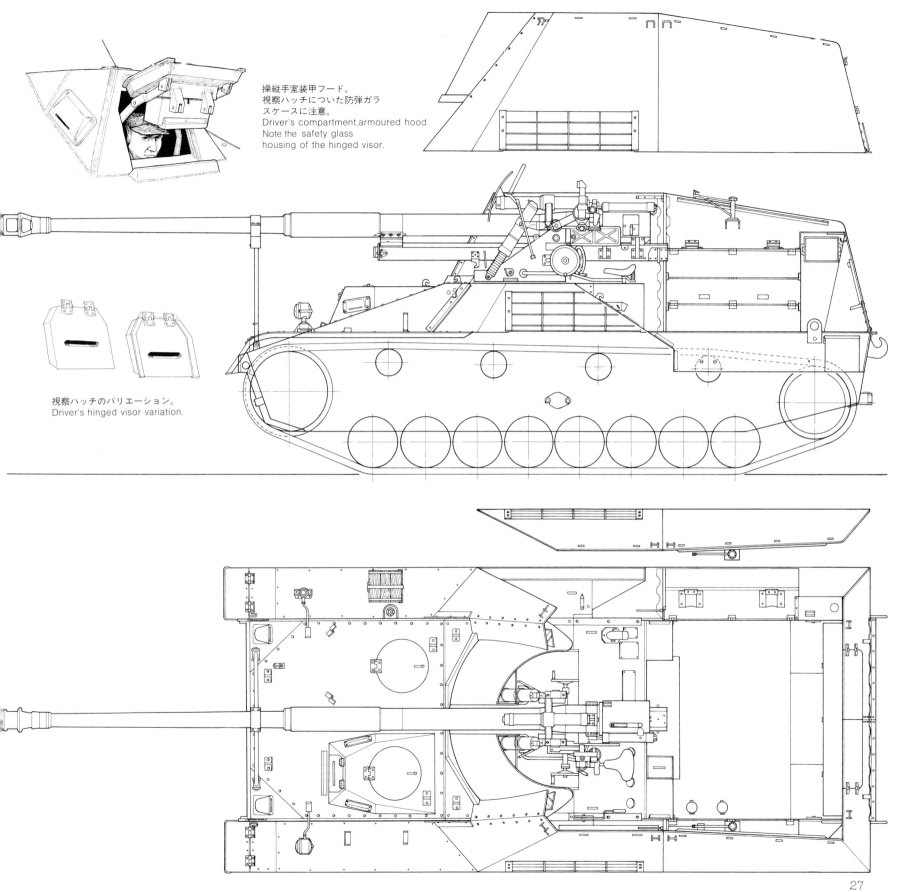

操縦手室装甲フード、
視察ハッチについた防弾ガラ
スケースに注意。
Driver's compartment,armoured hood
Note the safety glass
housing of the hinged visor.

視察ハッチのバリエーション。
Driver's hinged visor variation.

27

8.8cm Pak43/41 at Aberdeen Proving Ground
アバディーンの8.8㎝ Pak43/41

1

2

3

5

6

4

7

8

9

1. 砲操作ハンドル。俯仰ハンドルの真ん中についているのが発射ボタンである
Gun operating hand wheels. Note the trigger in the center of the elevating wheel.
2. 砲の反対側。補助砲俯仰ハンドルに注意
Other side of the gun. Note the auxiliary elevating hand wheel.
3. 駐鋤が折り畳まれて、砲は牽引姿勢にされている
Rear view of the gun. The trail recoil spades are in the folded position ready for towing.
4. 閉鎖器の左上部の角についているはずの閉鎖ブロック作動スプリングケースは失われている
Note breech mechanism spring case is missing from the port upper edge of the breech.
5. 右舷から見たPak43/41
Starboard side view.
6. 砲身直下にはトラベルクランプ、車輪の脇にはハンドブレーキレバーが見える。折り

畳んだ下部防盾にはスコップの取り付け金具がついている
Note the gun crutch just below the barrel. There is a hand brake lever beside the wheel. The spade bracket can be seen on the folded lower front shield.
7. トラベルクランプは外すと前方に倒れる
The gun crutch would hinge down forward when it would be released.
8. 防盾は二重になっている
Note the double layer type shield (spaced

armour)
9. この砲は砲脚は合わされ、駐鋤は砲脚の上に折り畳まれ、砲身はトラベルクランプで固定、下部防盾も跳ねあげられるなど、完全に牽引姿勢にされている
Pak43/41 ready for towing with trails together and the recoil spades carried on top of the trails, barrel fixed with crutch, lower front shield folded up.

8.8cmPak43/41重対戦車砲とナスホルン
8.8cm Pak43/41 heavy anti-tank gun and Nashorn

作図／小林源文　Drawn by Motofumi Kobayashi

8.8センチPak43/41重対戦車砲はPak43の砲身と、10.5センチ軽野榴弾砲18型の砲架と砲脚、そして15センチ重野戦榴弾砲18型の車輪から構成されていた。ナスホルンはこの砲の砲身と上部砲架をそのまま搭載している。この砲から発射される対戦車榴弾43/41は初速1,130メートル／秒、2,000メートルの距離から30度に傾斜した153ミリの圧延均質装甲板を貫通することができた。
A 8.8cm Pak43/41 anti-tank gun consisted of a Pak 43 barrel, 10.5cm leFH18's carriage and trail with 15cm sFH18's wheel. The Nashorn self propelled heavy anti-tank gun mounted a top carriage, cradle, and barrel of this gun. The Pzgr43/41 round of this gun had a muzzle velocity of 1,130m/s and could penetrate 153mm homogenous armour (30 degrees) at 2,000m.

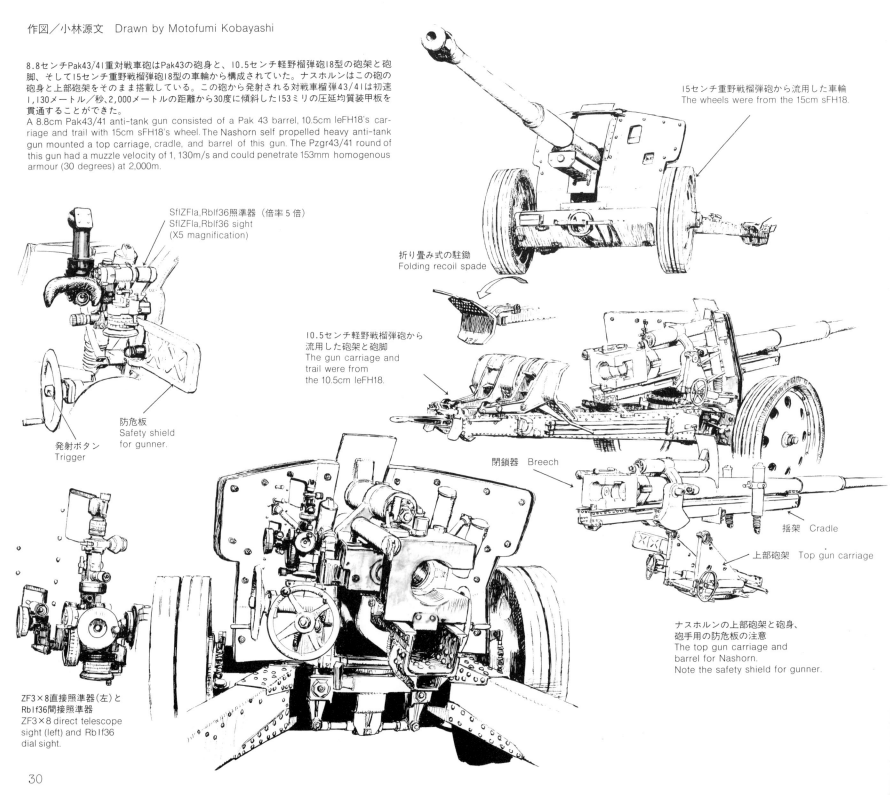

15センチ重野戦榴弾砲から流用した車輪
The wheels were from the 15cm sFH18.

SflZFla,Rblf36照準器 （倍率 5 倍）
SflZFla,Rblf36 sight
(X5 magnification)

折り畳み式の駐鋤
Folding recoil spade

10.5センチ軽野戦榴弾砲から
流用した砲架と砲脚
The gun carriage and
trail were from
the 10.5cm leFH18.

防危板
Safety shield
for gunner.

発射ボタン
Trigger

閉鎖器　Breech

揺架　Cradle

上部砲架　Top gun carriage

ナスホルンの上部砲架と砲身、
砲手用の防危板の注意
The top gun carriage and
barrel for Nashorn.
Note the safety shield for gunner.

ZF3×8直接照準器（左）と
Rblf36間接照準器
ZF3×8 direct telescope
sight (left) and Rblf36
dial sight.

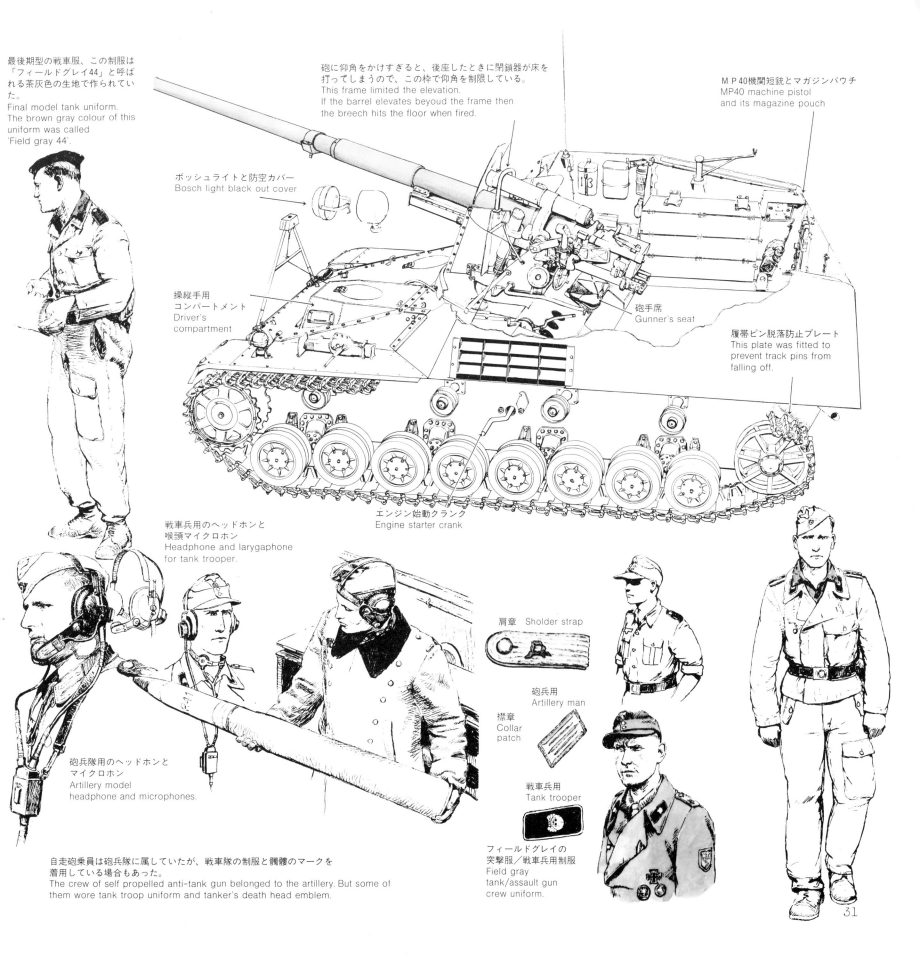

最後期型の戦車服、この制服は「フィールドグレイ44」と呼ばれる茶灰色の生地で作られていた。
Final model tank uniform. The brown gray colour of this uniform was called 'Field gray 44'.

砲に仰角をかけすぎると、後座したときに閉鎖器が床を打ってしまうので、この枠で仰角を制限している。
This frame limited the elevation. If the barrel elevates beyoud the frame then the breech hits the floor when fired.

ＭＰ40機関短銃とマガジンパウチ
MP40 machine pistol and its magazine pouch

ボッシュライトと防空カバー
Bosch light black out cover

操縦手用コンパートメント
Driver's compartment

砲手席
Gunner's seat

履帯ピン脱落防止プレート
This plate was fitted to prevent track pins from falling off.

エンジン始動クランク
Engine starter crank

戦車兵用のヘッドホンと喉頭マイクロホン
Headphone and larygaphone for tank trooper.

砲兵隊用のヘッドホンとマイクロホン
Artillery model headphone and microphones.

肩章　Sholder strap

砲兵用
Artillery man

襟章
Collar patch

戦車兵用
Tank trooper

フィールドグレイの突撃服／戦車兵用制服
Field gray tank/assault gun crew uniform.

自走砲乗員は砲兵隊に属していたが、戦車隊の制服と髑髏のマークを着用している場合もあった。
The crew of self propelled anti-tank gun belonged to the artillery. But some of them wore tank troop uniform and tanker's death head emblem.

31

8.8cmPak43/41at Leningrad Artillery Museum
レニングラード砲兵博物館の8.8cmPak43／41

1

2

3

4

5

6

7

8

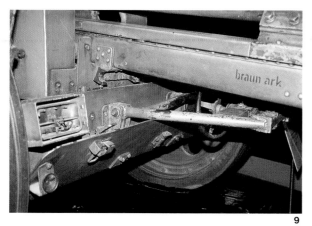

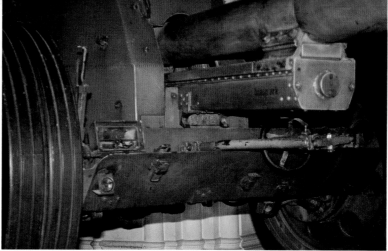

9

10

14

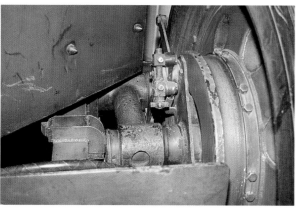

11

15

16

12

13

17

1. 砲の操作ハンドル。塗装は捕獲当時のままらしい
Gun operating hand wheels. Note the original colour of this gun.

2. 砲身と閉鎖器はパンツァーグレイ、他の部分はダークイエロー
The barrel and breech were painted Panzer gray. Other parts were painted Dark Yellow which had a very oily finished.

3. 砲俯仰機構
Gun elevating mechanism.

4. 防盾上にはハンマー取り付け金具がある
Note the hammer bracket on the shield.

5. Pak43／41の照準器。ZF3×8直接照準器マウント（左）とRblf36間接照準器（右）

The sights of Pak43/41. There is a ZF3×8 direct sight telescope mount (left) and a Rblf36 dial sight (right).

6. 閉鎖器。閉鎖ブロック中央の撃発機構のが抜き取られているのに注意
Gun breech. Note the firing mechanism cap is missing from the center of the breech block.

7. 砲俯仰ハンドルのグリップは木製である
Note the wooden hand grip of the auxiliary elevating hand wheel.

8. 別の方向から見た砲俯仰機構
Other side view of the gun elevating mechanism.

9. 車間表示燈の前面パネルは失われている、その下の反射板、折り畳まれたトラベルクラ

ンプ、揺架に入れられた「braun ark」の黒いステンシルに注意。これは「ブラウン駐退液」という意味
The front cover of the convoy light is missing. Note the reflector below the convoy light and folded gun crutch, black stencil'braun ark' on the cradle which means 'brown buffer fluid'.

10. 揺架と一体化された駐退管にはブラウン駐退液が充填されている。だが駐退液は極寒期には「極地駐退液」に交換される
The recoil brake cylinder incorporates a cradle and it was filled with 'brown buffer fluid' which was replaced by 'arctic buffer fluid' in conditions of serve cold.

11. 車軸とブレーキ機構

Wheel shaft and brake mechanism.

12. 砲脚と下部砲架
Joint of trail and under gun carriage.

13. 下部砲架の下側
Under side of lower gun carriage.

14. 俯仰ハンドルの真ん中に見える黒い発射ボタンに注意
Note the black trigger in the center of the elevating hand wheel.

15. 損傷している砲脚の先端
Damaged gun trail ends.

16. 下部砲架
Under carriage of the gun.

17. 左舷から見たPak43/41
Port side view of the gun.

33

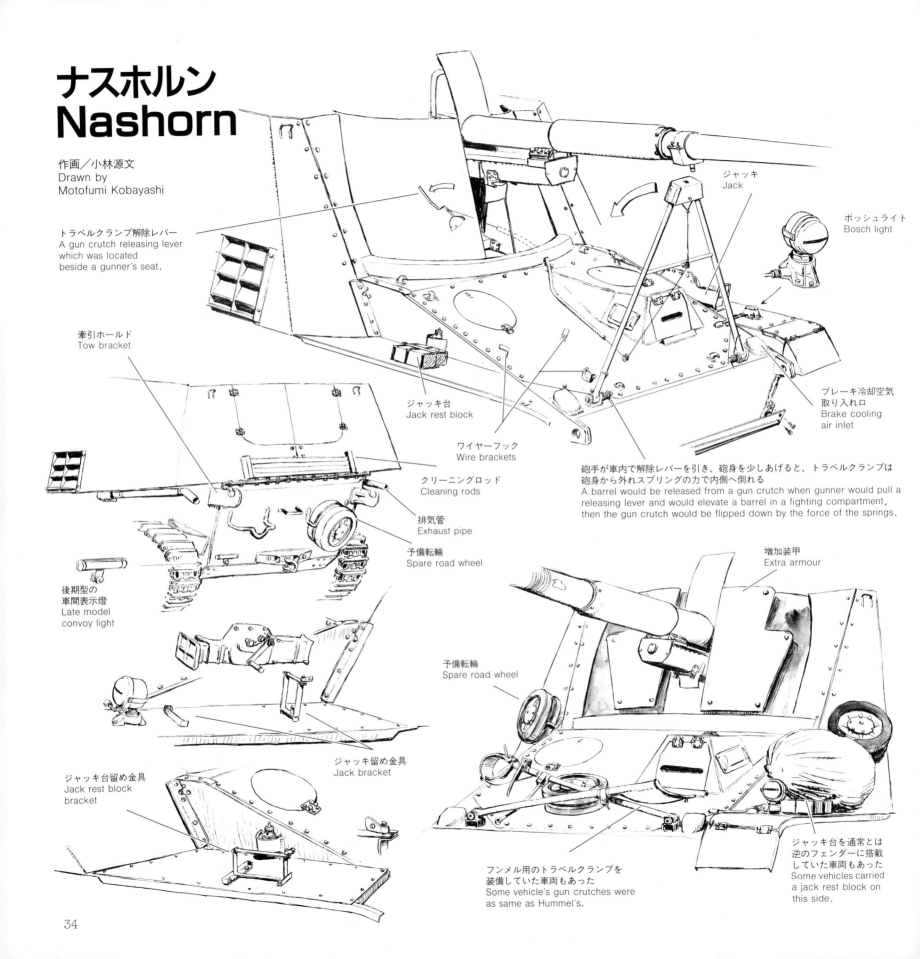

ナスホルン
Nashorn

作画／小林源文
Drawn by
Motofumi Kobayashi

トラベルクランプ解除レバー
A gun crutch releasing lever
which was located
beside a gunner's seat.

牽引ホールド
Tow bracket

ジャッキ
Jack

ボッシュライト
Bosch light

ジャッキ台
Jack rest block

ワイヤーフック
Wire brackets

クリーニングロッド
Cleaning rods

排気管
Exhaust pipe

予備転輪
Spare road wheel

ブレーキ冷却空気
取り入れ口
Brake cooling
air inlet

砲手が車内で解除レバーを引き、砲身を少しあげると、トラベルクランプは
砲身から外れスプリングの力で内側へ倒れる
A barrel would be released from a gun crutch when gunner would pull a
releasing lever and would elevate a barrel in a fighting compartment,
then the gun crutch would be flipped down by the force of the springs.

後期型の
車間表示燈
Late model
convoy light

増加装甲
Extra armour

予備転輪
Spare road wheel

ジャッキ留め金具
Jack bracket

ジャッキ台留め金具
Jack rest block
bracket

フンメル用のトラベルクランプを
装備していた車両もあった
Some vehicle's gun crutches were
as same as Hummel's.

ジャッキ台を通常とは
逆のフェンダーに搭載
していた車両もあった
Some vehicles carried
a jack rest block on
this side.

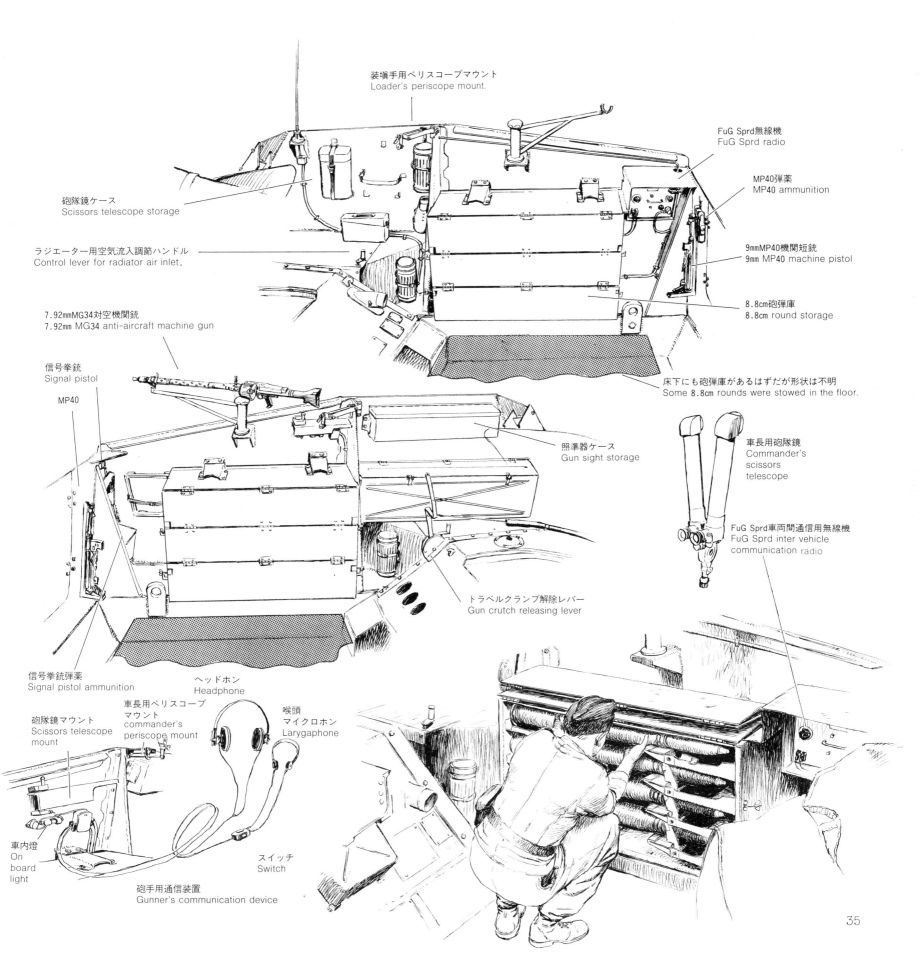

装填手用ペリスコープマウント
Loader's periscope mount.

FuG Sprd無線機
FuG Sprd radio

MP40弾薬
MP40 ammunition

9mmMP40機関短銃
9mm MP40 machine pistol

8.8cm砲弾庫
8.8cm round storage

砲隊鏡ケース
Scissors telescope storage

ラジエーター用空気流入調節ハンドル
Control lever for radiator air inlet.

7.92mmMG34対空機関銃
7.92mm MG34 anti-aircraft machine gun

床下にも砲弾庫があるはずだが形状は不明
Some 8.8cm rounds were stowed in the floor.

信号拳銃
Signal pistol

MP40

照準器ケース
Gun sight storage

車長用砲隊鏡
Commander's scissors telescope

FuG Sprd車両間通信用無線機
FuG Sprd inter vehicle communication radio

トラベルクランプ解除レバー
Gun crutch releasing lever

信号拳銃弾薬
Signal pistol ammunition

ヘッドホン
Headphone

喉頭マイクロホン
Larygaphone

砲隊鏡マウント
Scissors telescope mount

車長用ペリスコープマウント
commander's periscope mount

車内燈
On board light

スイッチ
Switch

砲手用通信装置
Gunner's communication device

Panzerjäger 38(t) mit 7.5cm Marder III

7.5cm Pak40対戦車自走砲38(t)マーダーIIIM型

このマーダーIIIは至るところサビが浮き出した状態ではあるが、車外の装備品はほぼ完全に残っており、きちんとした復元作業が行なわれれば、すばらしい状態になるだろう。

The MarderIII is awaiting restoration in the storehouse of the Saumur museum which is not opened to public.

Pak40/3 Ausf M (SdKfz138)

Manufacturer: BMM
Chassis Nos.: 2101–360

Crew: 4
Weight (tons): 10.5
Length (metres): 4.95
Width (metres): 2.15
Height (metres): 2.48

Engine: Praga AC
Gearbox: 5 forward, I reverse
Speed (km/hr): 42
Range (km): 190
Radio: FuG Spr d

Armament: One 7.5cm sPak40/3 L/46 One 7.92mm MG34
Traverse: 21° left 21° right(hand) loose
Elevation: −5° +13° loose
Sight: ZF3×8 direct
Ammunition: 27

Armour (mm/angle):	Front	Side	Rear	Top/Bottom
Superstructure:	10/30°	10/15°	10/0°	8/90°
Hull:	15/15°	15/0°	10/41°	10/90°
Gun shield:	6/28°	10/16°	10/17°	open

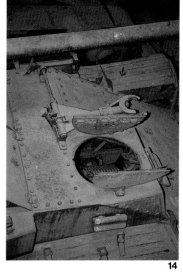

12　　　　**13**　　　　**14**

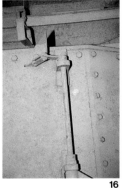

15　　**16**　　**17**　　**18**　　**19**

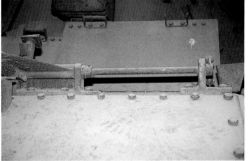

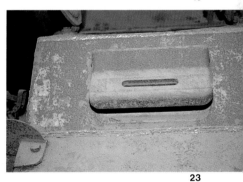

20　　　　**21**　　　　**22**　　　　**23**

1. 幌固定用の支柱
Hood support.

2. 上から見た砲防盾とエンジン点検ハッチ
Top view of gun shield and engine access hatches.

3. 幌固定用の支柱
Hood support.

4. 左舷フェンダー上の道具箱とジャッキ取り付け金具
Tool box and jack bracket on the port fender.

5. 戦闘室右舷の10mmリベット留め装甲板
Starboard 10mm riveted armour shield of fighting compartment.

6. この型の 6 mm砲防盾はマーダーシリーズ中もっとも薄いものであった
6mm rounded gun shield of this model which was the thinnest armour of the Marder series.

7. 左舷装甲板。砲を旋回させたときに照準孔をクリアできるように開けられた切り欠きに注意
Port armour shield. Note the cutting of the shield to clear the sight port when the gun traversed.

8. 車体左舷。車体の天辺にある砲クリーニングロッドの取り付け金具に注意
Port of the hull. Note the gun cleaning rod bracket on the hull top.

9. 半開きのエンジン点検ハッチ
Starboard half-opened engine access hatches.

10. 7.5cm Pak40の揺架カバー
7.5cm Pak40 gun cradle cap.

11. 半開きのエンジン点検ハッチ
Port half-opened engine access hatches.

12. ジャッキの取り付け金具は左舷フェンダーの道具箱と一体になっている。道具箱の蓋は失われている
The jack bracket incorporates the port punched tool box without the lid.

13. 砲防盾と機関室上部
Gun shield and engine deck.

14. 後期型（1944年）の熔接角型操縦コンパートメント。初期型は丸みのある鋳造装甲板で作られていた
Late(1944) model welded square driver's compartment armoured hood.The earlier model one had a rounded cast armoured hood.

15. ヘッドパッドがとれてしまった操縦手用ハッチ
The driver's hatch without the head protecting pad.

16. 上からジャッキ金具、クリーニングロッド金具、トラベリングロック操作用のシャフト。トラベリングロックは砲手が車内から解除することができた
From above,jack bracket,cleaning rod bracket and gun crutch operating shaft. It can be released with a lever in the fighting compartment by the gunner.

17. トランスミッション点検ハッチのある車体前部
Glacis with transmission access hatch.

18. 折り畳まれたトラベリングロック
Folded gun crutch.

19. 操縦用の覗視孔
Driver's hinged visor.

20. 左舷の工具取り付け金具
Port pioneer tool bracket.

21. トラベリングロック操作シャフト
Glacis and gun crutch operating shaft.

22. トラベリングロック
Gun crutch.

23. 操縦手用覗視孔
Driver's hinged visor.

1

2

3

4

5

6

7

8

9

10

11

12

13

14

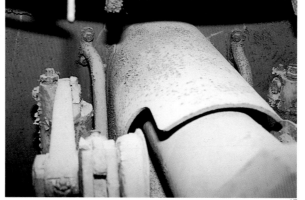

15

16

17　**18**　**19**　**20**

21

22

23

1.　戦闘室の左隅にある星型アンテナのマウントらしきものと、垂直式7.5cm砲弾庫に代わって設けられた大型無線機のラックに注意。本車はここにFuG8またはFuG4を搭載した指揮車両だったのかもしれない
Note the circular star rod aerial mount in the left corner of the fighting compartment and the larger radio rack replacing with the starboard vertical 7.5cm round storage. This vehicle might carry a FuG8 or a FuG4 radio set there when used as a command vehicle.

2.　後壁に折り畳まれている内装式の砲トラベリングロックに注意
Note the folded internal gun crutch on the rear wall.

3.　左舷の7.5cm砲弾庫。ここには12発の砲弾が垂直に搭載された。その後ろに見える後部のハッチのロックにも注目
Port 7.5cm round storage.There is 12 rounds stowed vertically.Note the rear wall door lock.

4.　砲左側を上から見たところ
Top view of port side of the gun.

5.　車両間通話用のFuG Sprd無線機のラック。その左側に乗員のガスマスクケース取り付け金具が見える
FuG Sprd inter vehicle communication radio set rack.The gas mask case bracket can be seen on the left side of it.

6.　7.5cm Pak40の閉鎖器
7.5cm gun breech.

7.　左舷7.5cm砲弾庫、戦闘中以外はキャンバスのカバーで覆われている
Port 7.5cm round storage which was covered with canvas top when not in action.

8.　左から、3発用砲弾庫（固定ベルトに注意）、消火器取り付け金具、蓋の開いた信号弾収納箱と砲手用の防危板
From left,rounds storage(note the retaining belts),fire extinguisher bracket,opened signal rounds storage box and safety shield for gunner.

9.　無線機ラックとその雨避け

Radio rack and its rain shield.

10.　砲の天井
Top cover of the gun.

11.　上から見た砲手位置
Top view of gunner's position.

12.　照準器ケースと消火器ラック、そして信号弾収納箱
The gun sight storage tube and the fire extinguisher bracket and the signal round storage box can be seen.

13.　砲防盾と照準器取り付け金具。ペリスコープマウントの一部も左上に見える
Gun shield and sight mount without sight.A part of the gunner's periscope mount can be seen above left.

14.　ZF 3×8 照準器は失われている
Gun sight mount,ZF3×8 sight is missing.

15.　7.5cm砲身の付け根を覆うカバー
7.5cm gun barrel and rounded cover on the shield.

16.　幌の支柱の中央についている対空機関銃マウント？

Anti-aircraft machine gun mount ?? on the hood support.

17.　7.5cm砲閉鎖器と防盾
7.5cm gun breech and the shield.

18.　砲操作ハンドル
Gun operating hand wheels.

19.　幌支柱の付け根と無線機の雨避け
The root of hood support and rain shield of radio.

20.　7.5cm砲の閉鎖器
7.5cmgun breech.

21.　装填手位置
Loader's position.

22.　砲の右側
The starboard side of the gun.

23.　幌の支柱（左）とFuG Sprアンテナ基部
Hood support(left) and FuG Spr Radio aerial mount.

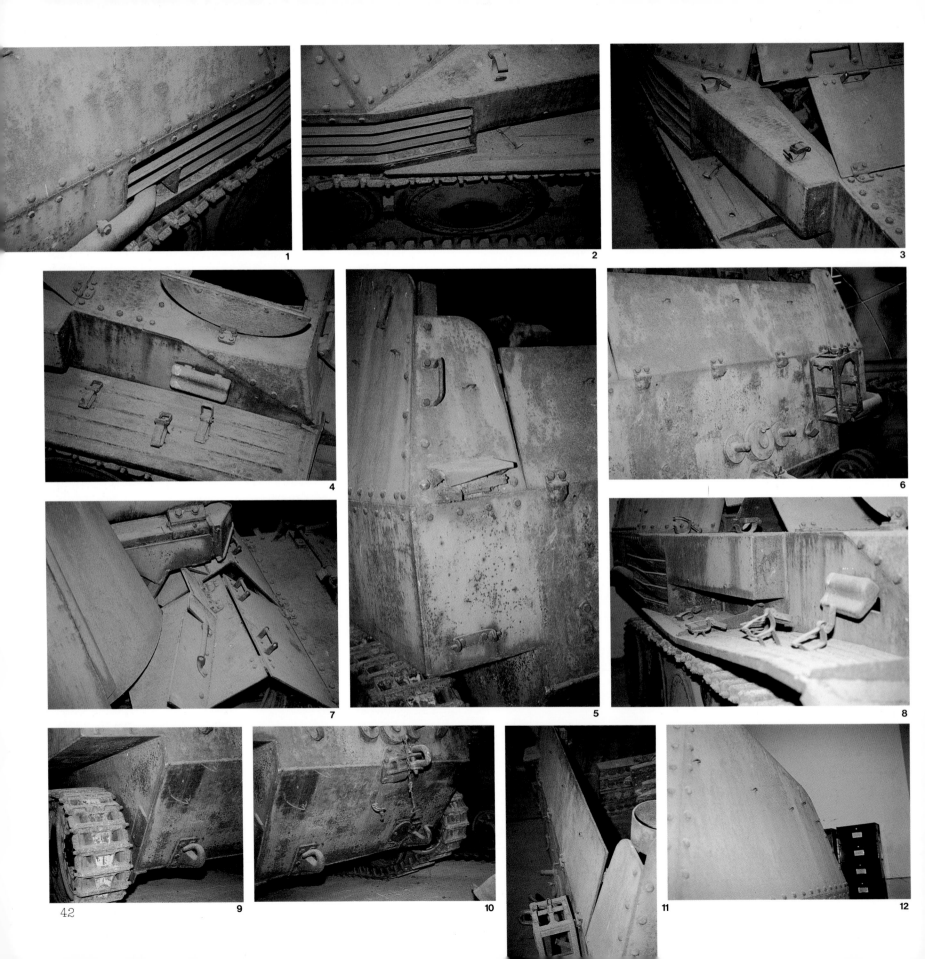

13

14

15

1. エンジン冷却気排出グリルと排気管
Engine cooling air outlet grill and exhaust pipe.

2. 右舷排気グリル。車体上に見える予備アンテナケース取り付け金具とフェンダー上の工具取り付け金具に注意
Starboard air outlet grill. Note the spare aerial storage tube bracket on the top of hull and pioneer tool bracket on the fender.

3. 予備アンテナケース取り付け金具
A pair of spare aerial storage tube brackets beside the engine deck.

4. フェンダー上の工具取り付け金具
Pioneer tool bracket on the starboard fender.

5. 戦闘室後部。上から乗り込み用把手、車間表示燈取り付け金具とカバー、乗り込み用ス

テップの取り付け跡（ステップ自体は失われている）
Rear wall of fighting compartment. From above, boarding handle, convoy light mount and its shield, boarding step base (step itself is missing).

6. 閉じられた戦闘室後部ハッチ。排気マフラーは失われている。無線機のラックがハッチのヒンジの一つに引っ掛けられているのに注意
Closing fighting compartment rear door. The exhaust muffler is missing. Note a radio rack is hanging at one of the hatch hinges.

7. 半開状態の機関室点検ハッチ
Half opened engine access hatchs.

8. 右舷フェンダー上の工具取り付け金具
Pioneer tools brackets on the starboard

fender.

9. 後部牽引フック
Rear tow bracket.

10. 後部の牽引ホールドと、一組の牽引フック、2個の牽引ロープフックとその留め金
A towing pintle, a pair of tow brackets, two cable hooks and clamp can be seen on the rear wall.

11. 後部ハッチについた小さな3つの幌用フックに注意。ハッチは外側に倒し、水平に固定することができた
Note the three tiny hooks for food on the rear door which can be hinged down and fixed horizontally.

12. 小さな4つの幌用フックがついている戦闘室側壁
Note the four tiny hooks for hood on the port fighting compartment wall.

13. アバディーンに展示されている車両。排気マフラーの下に、外部エンジンスターターとの接続アタッチメントが見える
This vehicle is displayed at Aberdeen proving ground. The engine starter device attachment plate can be seen just below the exhaust muffler.

14. アバディーンのマーダーⅢM型。予備覆帯があっちこっちについている
Aberdeen Marder Ⅲ ausf. M. Note that the spare tracks are on the glacis, lower hull front and both of the cheeks of the fighting compartment.

15. アバディーンのマーダーⅢM型。戦闘室前面に吊られた予備覆帯のフックに注目
Aberdeen Marder Ⅲ ausf. M. Note the hanger hooks of cheek spare track.

7.5cm Pak40/1auf Geschützenwagen Marder I

7.5cm Pak40対戦車自走砲ロレーヌ・シュレッパー(f)マーダーI

ソミュールには世界で唯一現存するフランス軍車両流用のドイツ軍自走砲が2両存在する。その1両がこのマーダーIであるが、残念ながらこの車両も非公開である。
The single surviving Marder I is at the Saumur museum. This vehicle is also not accessible to public.

Lorraine Schlepper (f) (SdKfz135)

Manufacturer: Alfred Becker
Chassis Nos.: 731001–

Crew: 5

Weight (tons): 8

Engine: DelaHaye 103TT
6cyl 3.55lit 70PS at 2,800rpm
Gearbox: 5 forward, I reverse
Speed (km/hr): 34
Range (km): 135
Radio: FuG5

Armament:	One 7.5cm Pak40/1L/46	One 7.92mm MG34
Traverse:	32 left 32 right(hand)	loose
Elevation:	−5° +22°	loose
Sight:	ZF3×8	direct

Armour (mm/angle):	Front	Side	Rear	Top/Bottom
Turret:	10/33	9/20	7/28	open
Superstructure:	9/35	9/45	9/35	6/90
Hull:	12/round	9/0	9/36	5/90
Gun shield:	10/33			

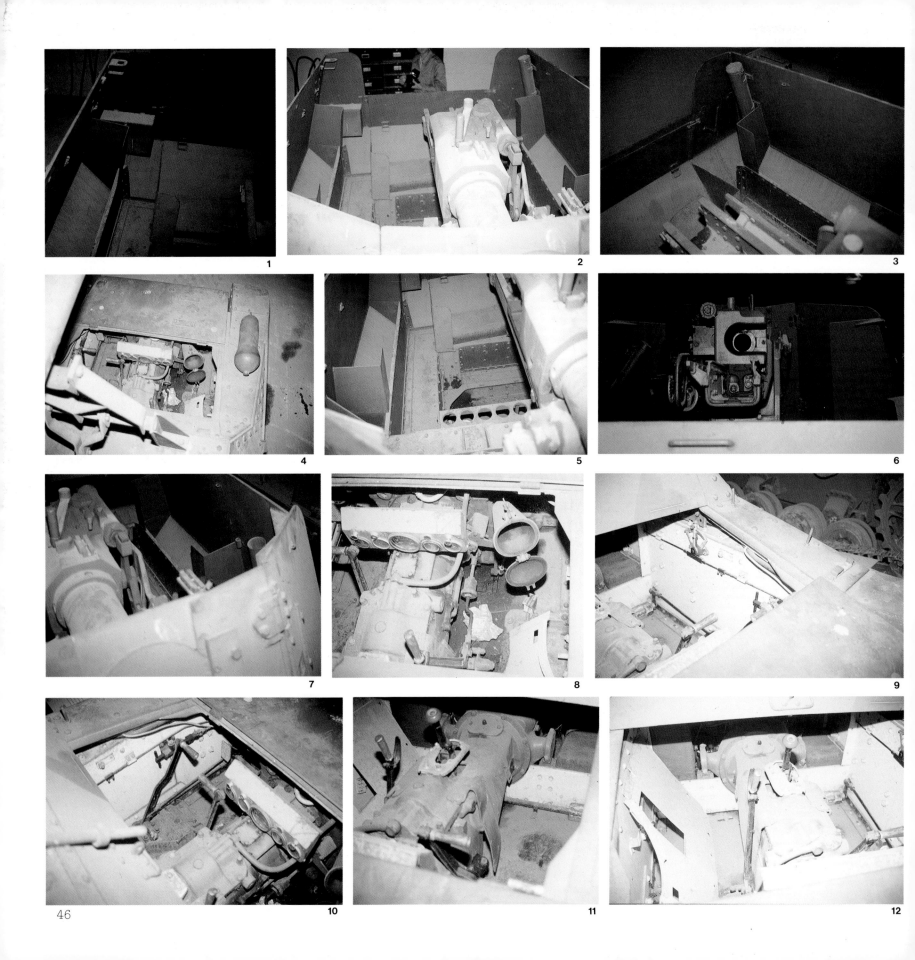

売上カード

㈱大日本絵画

パンツァーズ・アット・
ソミュール No.3

梅本弘、小林源文他・著

東京都千代田区神田錦町1の7
TEL 03・3294・7861
FAX 03・3294・7865

定価
(本体2,000円+税)

貴店名

補充をお忘れなくお願いします。

ISBN4-499-20597-2 C0076 ¥2000E

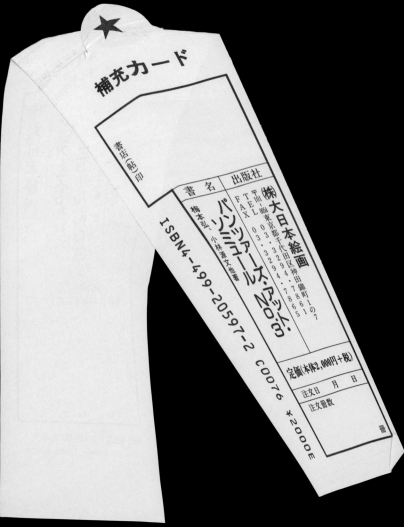

補充カード

書店(帖)印

出版社	書 名
㈱大日本絵画 〒101-0054 東京都千代田区神田錦町1の7 TEL 03・3294・7861 FAX 03・3294・7855	パンツァーズ・アット・ソミュール No.3 梅本弘、小林源文 他著

ISBN4-499-20597-2 C0076 ¥2000E

定価(本体2,000円＋税)

注文日　月　日

注文冊数　　　　冊

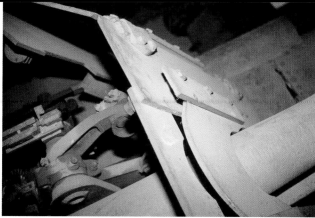

13

14

15

16

17

18

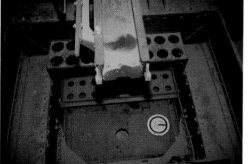

19

20

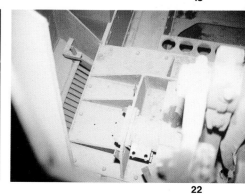

21

22

1. 戦闘室後部。アンテナ基部が隅に見える
Rear of fighting compartment. The aerial mount is in the corner.

2. 後部装甲板の前の乗員用ベンチに注目
Note the crew bench seat in front of the rear wall.

3. 後部ハッチは内側へ倒れる。小さくて簡単な掛金に注意
The rear door hinged down to the inside. Note the simple and tiny door latch.

4. 上から見た操縦手席
Top view of driver's compartment.

5. 7.5cm対戦車砲弾の縦型弾庫が砲の真下に見える
7.5cm anti-tank gun vertical round storage can be seen just below the gun.

6. 砲の防盾は砲の旋回に合わせて可動するようになっている
Inside view of hinged gun shield which

could spread for clear the gun traversing.

7. 側面装甲板に沿って作られたスペースには7.5cm砲弾が数発ずつ水平に搭載されたものと思われる
Some 7.5cm rounds were stowed horizontally in the racks on the both sides beside the side walls.

8. 変速機と計器盤が見える
The transmission and the instrument panel can be seen.

9. 操縦手席。横にツルハシの先端部を装着する取り付け金具が見える
Driver's position. Note the pick axe spike bracket on the glacis.

10. 操縦レバーとアクセルペダル
A pair of steering levers and the accelerator pedal can be seen in the driver's position.

11. 別角度から見た操縦手席。変速機の上のギ

アチェンジレバーが、横にはハンドブレーキが見える
Other side view of the driver's position. Note the gear change lever on the transmission and the hand brake beside it.

12. 別の角度から見た変速機
Other side view of the transmission.

13. 7.5cmPak40の照準器マウント。ZF 3 × 8 照準器は失われている
Gun sight mount of 7.5cm Pak40. ZF3×8 sight is missing.

14. 砲身の上の小防盾は砲の上下に沿って可動し、隙間が生じるのを防ぐ
Note the small movable shield on the barrel to cover the gap which would appear when the gun elevated.

15. 砲身とトラベルクランプ
Gun barrel and gun crutch.

16. 砲手用の防危板と砲操作ハンドル

Safety shield for gunner and gun operating hand wheels.

17. 開状態の砲閉鎖器
Note the open gun breech.

18. 砲直下のエンジン室
Engine compartment just below the gun mount.

19. 砲手位置
Gunner's position.

20. 砲直下の垂直式砲弾庫
Note the vertical 7.5cm Pak40 round storage just below the gun.

21. 装填手位置
Loader's position.

22. 別の角度から見た装填手位置
Other side view of the loader's position.

13

14

15

17

16

18

19

1. 砲防盾下部のすき間
The bottom gap of the gun shield.

2. エンジン室の天井
The top of the engine compartment.

3. 操縦手用の視察スリットと排気マフラー
The vision slits in the driver's compartment and exhaust muffler on the port side.

4. 定位置からずれているトラベルクランプ解除アームに注意。普段このアームの先端は砲の揺架キャップ下部に引っ掛かっており、砲に仰角をかけると外れ。トラベルクランプの上半分を前方に倒すように作られている
Note the flipped down gun crutch releasing arm, the hook of the arm was hung on the hold of the gun cradle cap and the arm forced to hinge down and the upper part of the crutch forward when the gun would elevate.

5. 変速機点検パネルの牽引ロープフックは一部破損している

There are broken tow cable hooks on the lower hull front transmission access panel.

6. 排気マフラー
Exhaust muffler.

7. マフラーの下にツルハシの柄を留める金具が見える
There are a pair of brackets for the pick axe handle just below the muffler.

8. エンジン冷却気吸入口
Engine cooling air inlet grill.

9. 起動輪付近
Around the drive sprocket.

10. 車体後部と誘導輪
Tail of the hull and idler wheel.

11. 車間表示燈の上につくはずのステップは失われてしまっている
The boarding step above the convoy light is missing.

12. 車体後部の用具入れ、蓋がなくなってしまっている

Tail of the hull. Note tail storage bin which is missing its lid.

13. 右舷フェンダーのフランス製防空燈。同車の大半はこの位置にジャッキを搭載し、防空燈は左舷フェンダーに移されている。また防空燈をノテック製の物に代えている車両も多い。さらにほとんどの車両が車体の先端上部に予備履帯を積んでいた。右舷の視察スリットが廃止されているのに注意
A French model blackout head light on the starboard fender. Most vehicle replaced the light with a jack and the French light was relocated to the port fender or replaced the with Notek light. Also all vehicle carried a spare track on the end of the glacis. Note the starboard vision slit was deleted.

14. 7.5cm Pak40の弾薬。シンチュウ色の弾頭と鉄色の薬莢に注意
7.5cm Pak40 ammunition, Note the steel colour case and brass projectole.

15. 7.5cm Pak40弾薬と、筒型の弾薬ケース
7.5cm Pak40 ammunition and its cylindrical metal canister.

16. 半開の乗員／変速機点検ハッチに注意
Note the half opened boarding/transmission access hatch in the glacis.

17. アバディーンの15cm sFH13(SF)GWロレーヌ・シュレッパー(f)の右舷エンジン点検ハッチ
Starboard engine access hatch of a 15cm sFH13(Sf)GWpLorraine Schlepper(f)of Aberdeen.

18. Pak40の閉鎖器と操作ハンドル、ZF3X8照準器に注意
Breech and operating hand wheels of Pak40. Note the ZF3X8 sight.

19. Pak40の閉鎖器
Breech of Pak40.

写真提供／斎木伸生

Leichte Feldhaubitze 18 / 2 auf Wespe

10.5cm軽自走榴弾砲　ヴェスペ

ヴェスペはドイツのコブレンツ、アメリカのアバディーン博物館にも保存されているが、いずれも保存状態はソミュールのヴェスペには及ばない。ただ残念なことにこの車両も今のところ非公開である。
This Wespe is also stored in the unopened store house of the museum.

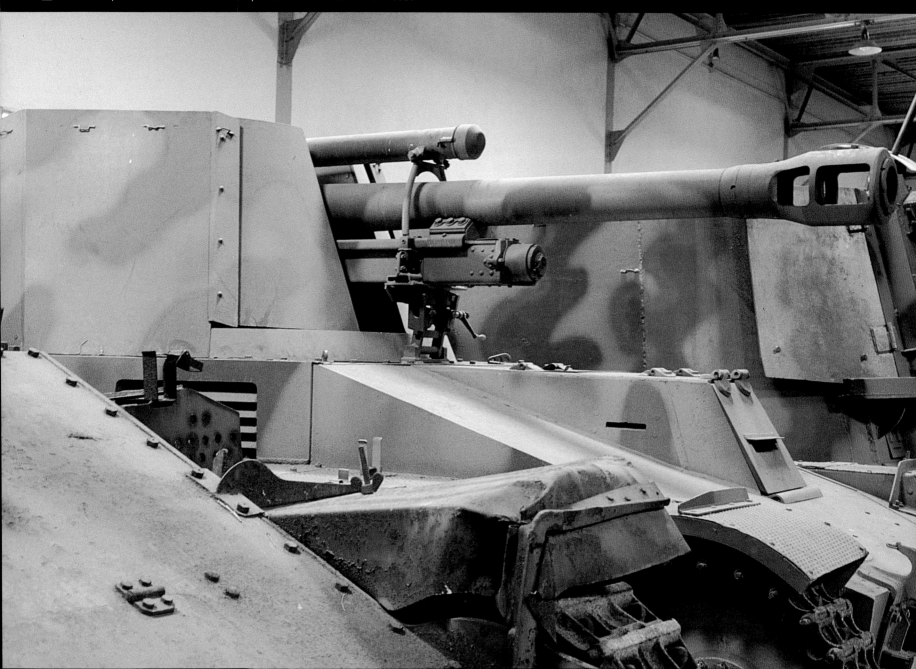

Fahrgestell Pzkpfw II (Sf)(SdKfz124)

		Armament:	One 10.5cm leFH18M L/28	One 7.92mm MG34	Armour (mm/angle):	Front	Side	Rear	Top/Bottom
Manufacturer: FAMO		Traverse:	17 left 17 right(hand)	loose	Superstructure:	20/30	15/0	8/0	10/90
Chassis Nos.: 31001–32190		Elevation:	−5 +42	loose	Hull:	30/15	15/0	15/10	5/90
Crew: 5	Engine: HL62TR	Sight:	Rblf36	direct	Gun shield:	10/24	10/17	10/16	open
Weight (tons): 11	Gearbox: 6 forward, l reverse	Ammunition:	32						
Length (metres): 4.81	Speed (km/hr): 40								
Width (metres): 2.28	Range (km): 220								
Height (metres): 2.3	Radio: FuG Spr f								

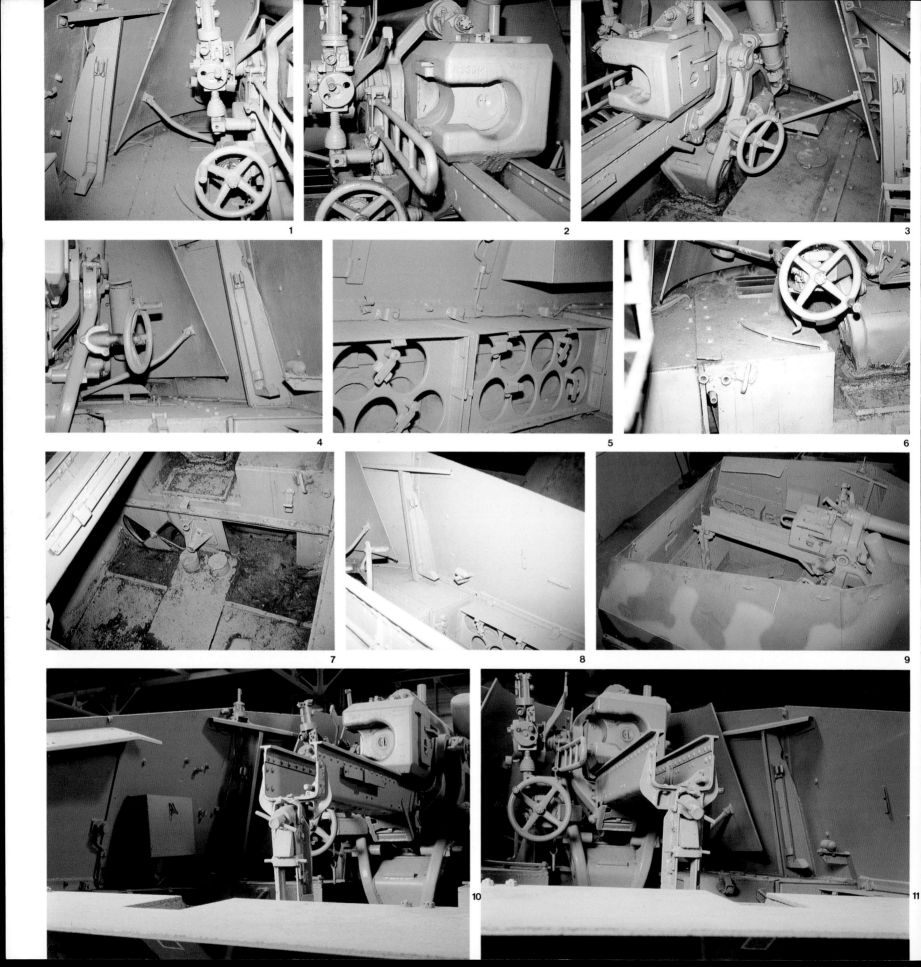

1

2

3

4

5

6

7

8

9

10

11

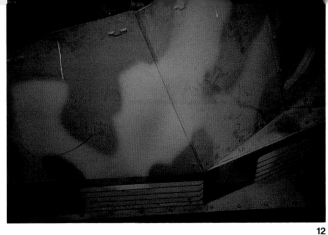

12　　　　　　　　　13　　　　　　　　　14

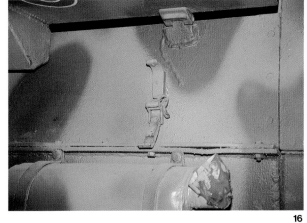
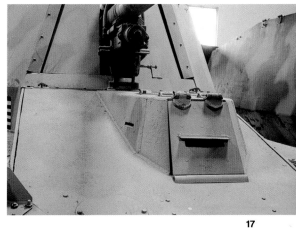

15　　　　　　　　　16　　　　　　　　　17

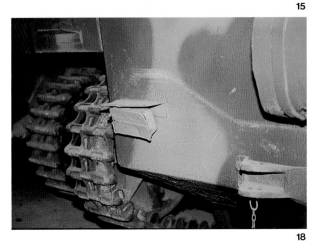
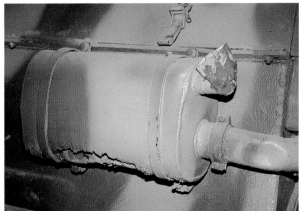

18　　　　　　　　　19　　　　　　　　　20

1. 砲手位置。丸みを帯びた砲防盾の傍らに
MP40機関短銃架とアンテナ基部がある
Gunner's position. The aerial mount and
the MP40 machine pistol bracket are
beside the rounded shield.
2. 10.5cmleFH18Mの閉鎖器とRblf36照準器
10.5cm leFH18M gun breech and Rblf36
sight.
3. 別の角度から見た砲
Another side view of the gun.
4. 上部砲架とMP40機関短銃架
Upper gun carriage and MP40 machine
pistol bracket.
5. 左舷10.5cm薬莢庫
Port 10.5cm round case storage.
6. エンジン室と砲操作ハンドル

Engine compartment and gun operating
hand wheel.
7. 戦闘室の床。二つの燃料注入孔に注目
The floor of fighting compartment. Note
the double fuel filler caps in the floor.
8. 右舷薬莢庫に注意
Note the starboard round case storage.
9. 無線機の雨避け、左舷薬莢庫と砲の内部ト
ラベルクランプが見える。後部ハッチは外側
に倒し、水平に固定することができた
The rain shield for the radio, port round
case storage and internal gun crutch can
be seen. The rear door hinged down to the
outside and it would fixed horizontally.
10. 水平に固定されている後部ハッチに注目
Note the rear door fixed horizonally.

11. 内部トラベルクランプの細部に注目
Note the internal gun crutch detail.
12. 戦闘室側面の幌フックに注意
Note the hood hooks on the side wall of
the fighting compartment.
13. 前面傾斜装甲と操縦手室用
Glacis and driver's compartment armoured hood.
14. 解除ハンドルのついた外部トラベルクラ
ンプ
External gun crutch with releasing crank
handle.
15. 車体後部、後部ハッチがハッチ外側の三
角形の突起によって水平にされているのがわ
かる
Tail of hull. The rear door is fixed horizon-

tally with a triangle bulge on the hatch.
16. 戦闘室と車体とのつなぎ目が見える
Joint of fighting compartment and hull.
17. 操縦手室とヒンジ付きの覗視孔、その下
には跳弾板も見える
Driver's compartment armoured hood with
hinged visor. Note the splash guard.
18. 牽引ホールドと車間表示燈
Tail tow bracket and convoy light.
19. 排気マフラー
Tail exhaust muffler.
20. 誘導輪のそばに見えるのは覆帯ピン脱
落防止プレート
The plate beside the idler is fitted to prevent the track pins from falling off.

53

10.5cm leFH18(Sf) auf Geschütz-

10.5cm18式軽自走榴弾砲　39H(f)

世界でこの博物館にだけ現存するフランス軍車台使用のドイツ軍自走砲、保存状態はかなり良い。
Saumur museum are storing only one survived 10.5cm le FH18(Sf) auf Geschützwagen 39H(f) in the world.

wagen Hotchkiss 39H(f)

Crew: 4
Weight (tons): 12.5

Engine: Hotchkiss 6cyl 6lit
120PS at 2,800rpm
Gearbox: 5 forward, 1 reverse
Speed (km/hr): 36
Range (km): 150
Radio: FuG Spr d

Armament: One 10.5cm leFH18L/28

Traverse: 30˚ left 30˚ right
Elevation: −5˚ +22˚
Sight: ZF3 × 8   Rblf36

One 7.92mm MG34
loose
loose
direct

Armour (mm/angle):	Front	Side	Rear	Top/Bottom
Turret:	20/30˚	20/10˚	10/25˚	open
Superstructure:	20/30˚	20/40˚	10/20˚	
Hull:	29-34/30˚	34/0˚	22/30˚	12/90˚
Gun shield:	20/30˚			

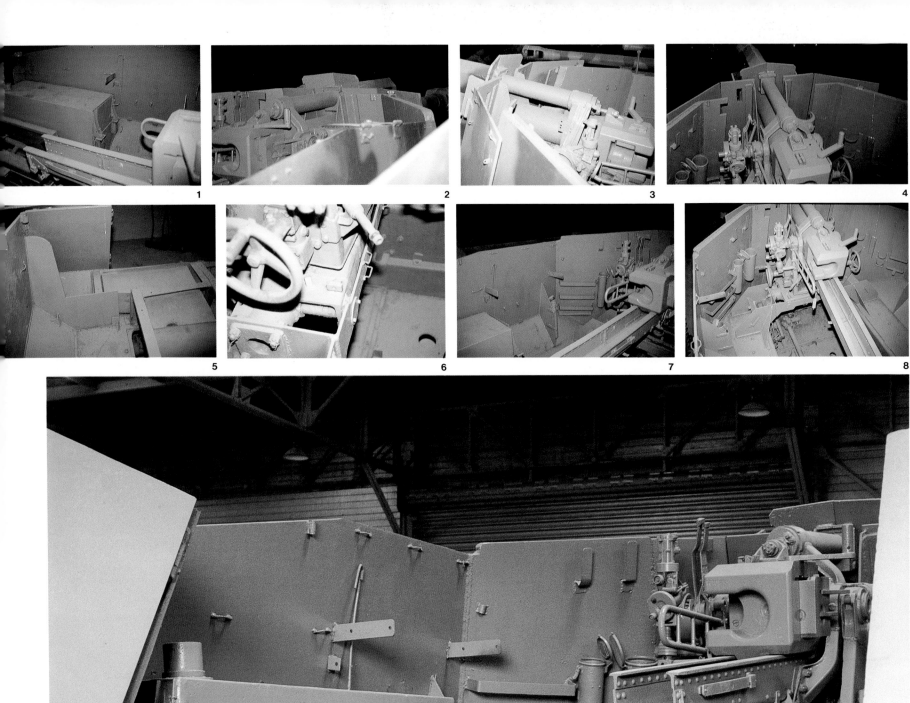

1 2 3 4

5 6 7 8

56

9

10

13

14

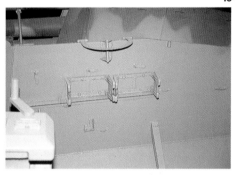

11

12

15

1. 角型の燃料タンクと天板のないエンジン室。10.5cm砲の薬莢はこの上に格納されていた。アンテナ基部が後部の角に見える
Square fuel tank and engine compartment without top cover. The 10.5cm round case stowed on the fuel tank. Note the aerial mount in the rear corner.

2. 10.5cm砲とその防盾
10.5cm gun and its shield.

3. ヒンジのついた砲防盾は砲の旋回に合わせて開くことができた
The hinged gun shield could be spread when the gun traversed.

4. 戦闘室前面の装甲板が二枚貼り合わせになっているのに注意
Note the double armoured cheek of the

fighting compartment.

5. エンジン室と10.5cm弾庫があったスペース
Engine compartment and 10.5cm round storage space.

6. 下部砲架。砲の旋回ハンドルが失われているのに注意
Lower gun carriage. Note the traverse hand wheel is missing.

7. 左から、燃料タンク、無線機ラックの跡、MG34の弾薬箱ラック。前面装甲板の上端に信号旗を挟むフックが見える
From left, fuel tank, radio rack and MG34 ammunition box bracket. Note the signal flag bracket on the top edge of the cheek armour.

8. 砲架の真下に動力伝達シャフトが見える
Drive shaft can be seen just below the gun mount.

9. 戦闘室左舷
Port side of the fighting compartment.

10. 右舷のMG34機関銃架基部？とそのドラム弾倉ラック？
Starboard MG34 machine gun mount base ? and its drum magazine storage ?

11. MG34機関銃架のスイングアームは失われ基部だけが残っている
MG34 mounting swing arm is missing from the base.

12. この博物館の倉庫の外に展示されている10.5cm砲
10.5cm gun which is displayed outside of

the warehouse of this museum.

13. 戦闘室右舷
Starboard of the fighting compartment.

14. 砲の右側についている補助俯仰ギア
Auxiliary elevating hand wheel on the starboard of the gun and elevating gear.

15. 戦闘室とエンジン冷却空気取り入れ口のグリル
Fighting compartment and engine cooling air intake grill of the tail.

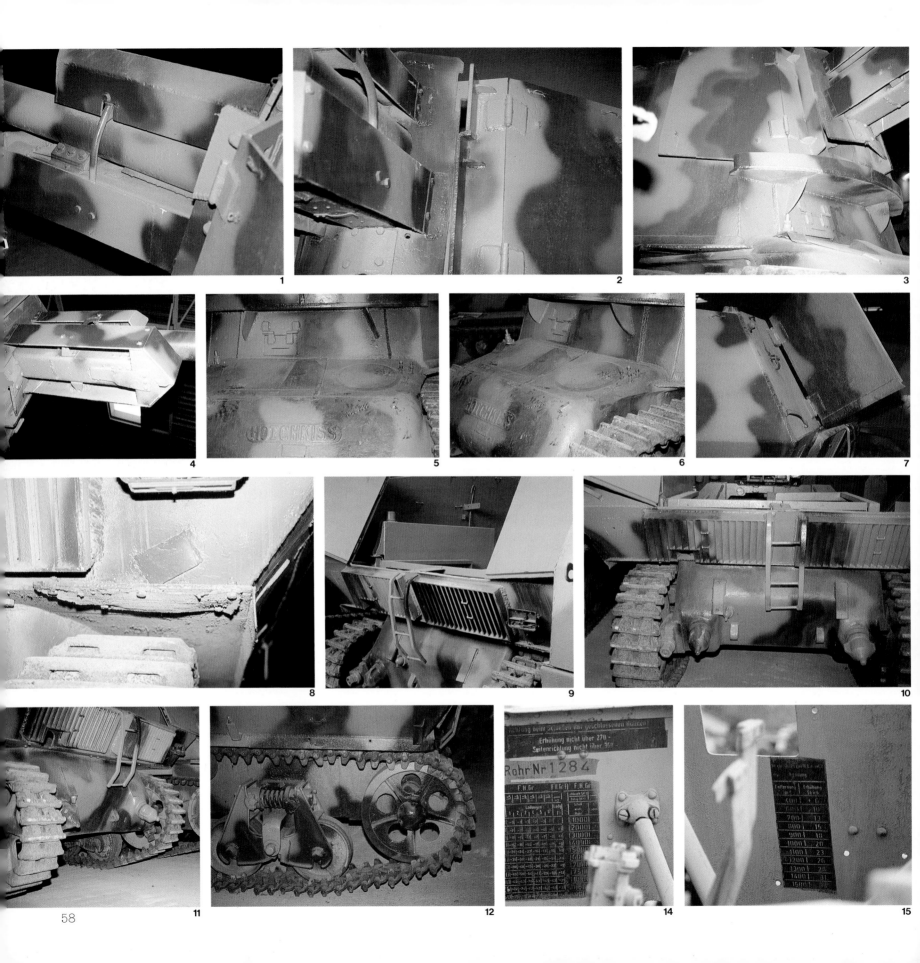

1. 10.5cm砲身と、駐退復座器の装甲ガード
10.5cm gun barrel and armour protector for the recuperator cylinder and cradle.
2. 砲が旋回するときには開くようになっているヒンジ付き防盾
Note the hinged gun shield which could be spread when the gun traversed.
3. ヒンジ付きの防盾と駐退復座器ガード。操縦手用のヒンジ付覗視孔とノテックライトの基部に注意
Hinged gun shield and recoil mechanism protectors. Note the driver's hinged visor and Notek light mount.
4. 下から見た揺架とその装甲ガード
Underside view of cradle armour protec-

tor.
5. 熔接構造のドイツ製上部構造物が鋳造製のオチキスの車体に載っている
The German welded superstructure is on the French Hotchkiss H39 cast hull.
6. 両側のフェンダーとフランス製防空燈は失われている。左舷のフェンダーには予備転輪が、右舷には予備覆帯が搭載されていた
Both fenders and a French model blackout light are missing. This vehicle was carrying the spare track links on the port fender and a spare wheel on the starboard.
7. 戦闘室後部
Rear of the fighting compartment.
8. 車体後部の泥避けは失われている

The tail mud flap is missing.
9. 排気マフラー、車間表示燈の前面カバーなどは失われている
The tail exhaust muffler is missing. The front cover of the convoy light is also missing.
10. マフラーは乗降ハシゴの内側についていた。マフラー架取り付け金具の跡に注意
The muffler was positioned inside the boarding step. Note the muffler support lugs.
11. 覆帯緊張装置が誘導輪のそばに見える
The track tenision adjustment device can be seen beside the far idler wheel.
12. 誘導輪と転輪。カナテコの取り付け金具が覆帯のすぐ上に見える

Idler wkeel and road wheel. Note the crow-bar bracket on the track guard.
13. 車体下部前面に牽引ロープの取り付けフックがついていた跡が見える
Note the marks of tow cable hooks on the nose of lower hull.
14. 10.5cm砲の防盾内側に貼られた装薬表
The loading table on a 10.5cm gun shield.
15. 防盾内側の仰角表
The elevation table on a gun shield.

■弊社出版物ご購入ご希望の方は、書店の店頭でご注文なさるか（この場合送料はかかりません）、右記まで直接、定価（表示の価格は全て税込価格です）に送料を添えて現金書留か普通為替、郵便切手にてお申し込み下さい。　　〒101 東京都千代田区神田錦町1-7　㈱大日本絵画　MG係　Phone 03-3294-7861（代表）

パンツァーズ・アット・ソミュールNo.1新装版
小林源文／梅本 弘著　2,000円

ISBN4-499-20543-3

ソミュール戦車博物館のコレクションからティーガーII、IV号戦車L70、ルックスを選んで取材。実車ディテール写真は全てカラー、他にもイラスト、図面を多数掲載している。

パンツァーズ・アット・ソミュールNo.2
小林源文／梅本 弘著　2,000円

ISBN4-499-20554-9

世界最大を誇るソミュール戦車博物館のコレクションから復元状態の良いドイツ戦車パンターA型、パンツァーベルファー42、ヤークトパンターを選んで、その外／内部を詳細に撮影。

パンツァーズ・アット・ソミュールNo.3
小林源文／浪江俊明／梅本 弘著　2,000円

ISBN4-499-20597-2

フンメル、ナスホルン、Pak43の細部写真や1:35図面、細部イラスト等を中心に、非公開の珍しいドイツ自走砲車種を徹底取材。

アハトゥンク・パンツァーNo.2
尾藤満他著　2,000円

ISBN4-499-20578-6

III号戦車フルバリエーションの細部を精密な線画で克明に分析。また各国に現存する車両のカラー細部写真と1:35スケール図面も併載。

アハトゥンク・パンツァーNo.3
尾藤満他著　2,500円

ISBN4-499-22621-X

新たな資料をもとにしたIV号戦車資料の決定版。未発表多数と、大戦中の実車写真と、富岡吉勝氏作図／解説による1:35IV号戦車各型基本寸法を新たに追加。

アハトゥンク・パンツァーNo.4
尾藤満他著　2,800円

ISBN4-499-22671-6

パンター、ヤークトパンター、ブルムベアの各型の細部を詳しく描いた線画を中心に、1:35の4面図、世界各国の博物館に現存している車両の細部カラー写真などを満載。

アハトゥンク・パンツァーNo.5
尾藤満他著　3,400円

ISBN4-499-22654-6

O型からG型に至るIII号突撃砲と、IV号突撃砲、そして15センチ砲を搭載した重突撃歩兵砲33B等の線画と図面、ドイツ軍の操作教本、現存する実車の車内、車外の細部カラー写真等を掲載。

パンツァーファイル'97〜'98
月刊『モデルグラフィックス』編集部・編　3,900円

ISBN4-499-22674-0

世界中のドイツAFVキットを完全網羅したスーパーカタログ「パンツァーファイル」最新版。1:35スケールキットとして問屋や相信店を経て流通しているものなら、もれなく収録しています。

モデルズ・イン・アクション1ノルマンディ
2,900円

ISBN4-499-22639-2

ノルマンディ上陸作戦とそれにつづく、北フランスでの戦闘を、驚くほど完成度で作られた1:35から、1:6の10個もの大型ダイオラマで再現した写真作品集。

モデルズ・イン・アクション2ベルリン
3,500円

ISBN4-499-22660-0

好評のシリーズの第2弾。第三帝国最後の戦闘、ベルリンの戦いをテーマにダイオラマ作品集。今回も1:16から1:35までの大型作品10個で構成されている。

日本の軍装　改訂版
中西立太著　2,900円

ISBN4-499-20587-5

日中戦争〜太平洋戦争終結までの日本陸海軍の軍装の全て。

日本の歩兵火器
中西立太著　2,800円

ISBN4-499-22690-2

日中戦争、太平洋戦争で使用された帝国陸軍の火器を完全図解。

フリーガーファイル'94〜'95
月刊モデルグラフィックス編集部編　2,816円

ISBN4-499-22640-6

ドイツ軍用機模型カタログ。デカール類のフォローも完璧。

パンツァー・ユニフォーム
M・ブルット著　4,175円

ISBN4-499-22649-X

第二次大戦のドイツ陸軍機甲部隊制服のすべてを、多数の写真図版を駆使して解説。公文書に残る制式軍装ばかりでなく、旧軍人へのインタビューによって判明した非公式軍装も紹介。

重戦車大隊記録集1・陸軍編
W・シュナイダー著　5,800円

ISBN4-499-22668-6

第二次大戦中活躍したティーガー戦車大隊各部隊の戦闘記録および、未発表多数含む700枚以上もの戦場写真を中心に、各部隊ごとのマーキング、迷彩のカラー図も掲載。

ドイツの自動火器
ロバート・ブルース著　3,800円

ISBN4-499-22682-1

第二次大戦中にドイツ軍が使用した自動火器の取扱や射撃を通じて、その実像を浮かび上がらせるという異色の研究書。

世界の駄っ作機
岡部ださく著　2,400円

ISBN4-499-22689-9

『月刊モデルグラフィックス』に大人気連載中のコラムが、一冊の本になりました。航空史の裏を適当に彩る駄目飛行機、ここに集う。

雪中の奇跡
梅本弘著　2,800円

ISBN4-499-20536-0

1939年11月、150万もののソ連軍部隊がフィンランド国境を越えた。ところが侵入した連隊団は一つまた一つと全滅していった。いったい雪深いフィンランドの森で何が起ったのか？

パンツァーズ・イン・ノルマンディ
E.Lefevre著　3,900円

ISBN4-499-20527-1

1944年、ノルマンディに上陸した英米連合軍を迎え撃ったドイツ軍戦車隊の記録を各戦車連隊／独立大隊ごとに多数の写真、図版、地図を駆使して克明に掲載。

ドイツのロケット彗星
ヴォルフガング・シュペーテ著　2,233円

ISBN4-499-22623-6

ドイツ空軍戦闘機パイロットとして99機撃墜のスコアをあげた著者が克明に描きあげた世界唯一のロケット戦闘機の開発、そして実戦場におけるエピソード。

アドルフ・ガラント
ヴェルナー・ヘルト著　2,524円

ISBN4-499-22615-5

ドイツ空軍のスーパーエースにして戦闘機総監、アドルフ・ガラント空軍中将。少年時代、実戦デビュー、戦闘機隊総監としての勤務、そして戦後の姿までを綴る。

ティーガーの騎士
カール・コーラッツ著　2,400円

ISBN4-499-22611-2

史上最大の戦車エース、ミヘル・ヴィットマンSS大尉の半生記。戦歴ばかりではなく人間的な側面も描かれている。未亡人から提供された未発表写真も掲載。

鉄十字の騎士
G・ウィリアムスン著　2,136円

ISBN4-499-22652-X

第二次大戦、騎士十字章を授けられたドイツ陸軍、空軍、海軍そしてSSの将兵、数十名を取り上げ、彼らの経歴、歴戦などを記述。また騎士十字章自体の解説、受章者一覧表も掲載。写真多数。

ティーガー戦車隊（上）（下）
オットー・カリウス著　（上）2,400円（下）2,330円

（上）ISBN4-499-22645-7
（下）ISBN4-499-22653-8

撤退を続けるドイツ陸軍の後衛として苦悩するティーガー中隊の戦い。やがて負傷したカリウス少尉は本国に戻り、騎士十字章を授けられ、ヤークトティーガー中隊の指揮を任せられることになる。

バルジの戦い（上）（下）（上、品切れ中）
ジャン・ピエール・パリュ著　（下）3,786円

（下）ISBN4-499-22610-4

第二次大戦におけるドイツ軍最後の大反攻作戦「アルデンヌ攻勢」を膨大な資料と、綿密な現地調査、米独両軍の生き残り将兵へのインタビューをもとに、完璧に再現。

UボートⅦ型 ドイツ潜水艦テクノロジーの全容
ロバート・C・スターン著　2,913円

ISBN4-499-22656-2

Uボートの中でも、主力艦として活躍したⅦ型に的を絞り、詳細に記述した最高の書物。

パンツァー・フォー
K・アルマン著　2,900円

ISBN4-499-20519-0

第二次大戦中、北アフリカ、ロシア、そして欧州の戦場を制し、思う存分暴れ回ったドイツ軍の戦車エースたちの戦いを克明に記録。

ティーガー（上）（下）
E・クライネ、V・キューン著　（上）2,913円（下）2,800円

（上）ISBN4-499-20563-8
（下）ISBN4-499-20571-9

世界最強と言われたティーガーの生い立ちから戦場での戦いぶりを、元戦車兵からのインタビューをもとに各独立重戦車大隊ごとに記録した迫真のドキュメント。

わたしは零戦と戦った
J・フォスター著　2,718円

ISBN4-499-22628-7

コルセアを駆り、ソロモン群島で日本海軍機と死闘を交えた著者の空戦記録。その記述は戦いのみならず、基地での生活にも及び、その筆致は具体的で生彩に溢れている。

ストーミング・イーグルス
ジェイムズ・ルーカス著　3,204円

ISBN4-499-22606-6

実際に降下猟兵と戦った経験をもつ著者が、多数の元降下猟兵にインタビューして作り上げた臨場感溢れるドキュメント。写真多数。

エーリッヒ・ハルトマン
ウルスラ＆エーリッヒ・ハルトマン著　3,495円

ISBN4-499-20534-4

ドイツ空軍のエース・パイロット、エーリッヒ・ハルトマンの写真集。新兵時代、ソ連軍との激戦、そして戦後10年にわたるソ連での収容所生活などを記録。

パンツァーモデリング・マスタークラス
トニー・グリーンランド著　2,800円

ISBN4-499-22681-3

ドイツ戦車模型のエキスパートとして世界的に有名なイギリスのトニー・グリーンランドが、その卓越したテクニックを自ら紹介、解説した、戦車模型ファン待望の日本語版。

SS戦車隊（上）（下）
ヴィル・フェイ著　各2,900円

（上）ISBN4-499-22627-9
（下）ISBN4-499-22630-0

SS第102重戦車大隊の戦車長としてノルマンディ戦に参加した著者が自分自身の経験と各SS重戦車連隊で戦った中隊長、戦車長、砲手、操縦手などの手記を編集。

空対空爆撃戦隊
ハインツ・クノーケ著　2,233円

ISBN4-499-20600-6

大空に憧れ空軍に入隊した少年。ある日、かれは戦友とともに案出した空対空爆撃戦術で米四発重爆を撃墜、やがてそれはロケット弾を使った戦術に発展した。

ドイツ空軍の終焉
ヴェルナー・ジービッヒ著　2,427円

ISBN4-499-22633-X

西部戦線におけるドイツ空軍戦闘機隊最後の奮戦を写真と具体的なデータをあげて詳述。とくに「ボーデンプラッテ作戦」に関する詳細な記述は本書ならではのものである。

ティーガー重戦車写真集
富岡吉勝監修　2,700円

ISBN4-499-22688-2

フランス公文書館ECPAに保存のオリジナルネガから、ティーガーをメインテーマに撮影した、写真100枚以上を選んで、ネガナンバー順に収録。巻末には戦記劇画の第一人者である小林源文氏の「ティーガー・フィーベル」も掲載。

ドイツ軍用車両戦場写真集
富岡吉勝監修　2,800円

ISBN4-499-22693-7

ドイツ軍部隊の最前線に従軍したカメラマンが残した写真をネガナンバー順に連続収録。各写真の撮影時期と場所、所属部隊のデータにもこだわっている。

グロースドイッチュラント師団写真史
トーマス・マックギール＋レミーズベツァーノ著　3,000円

ISBN4-499-22697-X

完全に機械化され装備優良なエリート部隊「グロースドイッチュラント」。本書は新たに発見された多数の写真ネガを主に用い、かつての同師団の兵士の多方面からの解説文を加えた、信頼度の高い第一級の本である。

流血の夏
梅本 弘著　3,800円

ISBN4-499-22702-X

夜が訪れることのない北欧の夏。圧倒的な兵力をもってロシア軍の進撃によって、南部フィンランド全域の占領も間近と思われたそのとき、全予備兵力を結集したフィンランド軍による乾坤一擲の大反撃が発起される。

小社の出版物をご購入希望のかたは、お近くの書店にご注文ください。書店にない場合は、表示価格に消費税を加え、送料をそえて現金書留か、普通為替か切手で小社まで直接ご注文ください。送料は1回のご注文で1〜3冊までが240円、4冊以上の場合は小社で負担いたします。

注文・問い合わせ先
〒101-0054 東京都千代田区神田錦町1の7
㈱大日本絵画　MG係　☎03(3294)7861

★表示価格に消費税が加わります★

●Books with English/Japanese captions　＊Japanese version of foreign book(Japanese only).　＊＊Comic books in Japanese only.